Tasty Ideas From An
Accidental Home Cook

Tasty Ideas From An Accidental Home Cook

Cynthia Dawson

Cookbook Press   Page, Arizona

To contact the author or
order additional copies of this book
steelerfn26@hotmail.com

This edition was prepared for printing by
Ghost River Images
5350 East Fourth Street
Tucson, Arizona 85711
www.ghostriverimages.com

Cover design by: Cynthia Dawson

ISBN 978-0-615-51253-2

Library of Congress Control Number: 2011912063

Printed in the United States of America
Second Printing: September, 2011
10 9 8 7 6 5 4 3 2 1

Contents

Tips About This Book 1

Section 1 - Appetizers 5

Section 2 - Breakfast 29

Section 3 - Sandwiches & Salads 41

      Sandwiches: 42

      Salads: 64

Section 4 - Main Dishes 79

      Beef Dishes: 80

      Poultry Dishes: 93

      Pork Dishes: 114

Section 5 - Seafood & Fish 127

      Seafood: 128

      Fish: 141

Section 6 - Sides & Sauces 153

      Sides: 154

      Sauces: 175

To my husband Steve who believed in me
and did not let me give up on myself.
You are truly the best!

Tips About This Book

There are some recipes that have tips about the recipe whether it is how to make the dish, if it is a spicy dish, or how to deal with flare ups during grilling. There are recipes that have directions on certain ingredients that need to be made a head of time. Each recipe has the number of serving such as 4-6 serving this is base how big the portions are served. An example would be by serving small portions then a person should get six servings out of the recipe or serving larger portions would lead to four servings.

The recipes are written to were the ingredients call for prep work all ready done such as ¼ cup diced onion or ½ cup diced red bell pepper. Be sure to read the whole recipe to know what ingredients is needed and how they should be prepared. There are some recipes that call for tablespoons or teaspoons of diced onion or bell pepper which leads to this tip: diced up the onion or bell pepper then use a tablespoon to measure them for the recipe. The reason behind this was to make it easier for recipes that require less then a ¼ cup instead of saying one ounce using tablespoons was easier.

The recipes in this book are pretty simple recipes but there are some that have a lot of ingredients but do not be discourage because the recipe is still not that difficult to make. The ingredients used in these recipes a person should be able to find easily. The baking times in the book can vary based on oven and altitude so make sure to cook dishes until cooked through. There are some recipes that call for use of wine but it could be left out if one would like. That is all the tips there are before reading this book so please read on and have fun in the kitchen using the recipes that an accidental home cook came up with enjoy.

Temperature Cooking Chart

Food Item	Internal Temperature Degrees Fahrenheit
Beef (Steak)	
Rare	125-130 degrees F
Medium-Rare	130-140 degrees F
Medium	140-150 degrees F *
Medium-Well	150-160 degrees F
Well Done	Over 160 degrees F
Ground Beef	160 degrees F *
Poultry	
Chicken	165 degrees F *
Turkey	165 degrees F *
Pork (Steaks & Chops)	160 degrees F *
Ground Pork	160 degrees F *
Fish	145 degrees F *

* These temperatures are recommended safe minimum internal temperatures. The recommended safe minimum internal temperature for steak is 145 degrees F.

Section 1

Appetizers

Spicy Squares – Makes 10-12 wontons

- **10-12 wonton wrappers**
- **¼ pound regular pork chorizo**
- **¼ cup fresh grated parmesan cheese**
- **1 avocado (diced)**
- **1 (16ounce) container of sour cream**
- **1 package ranch seasoning**
- **2 ½ teaspoons oil**

Tip
This is a spicy dish.

Make Ahead
Mix 1 package of ranch seasoning with the 16 ounce container of sour cream until mixed in completely. Add the diced avocado to mix with fork to make sure avocado is mixed in completely. Chill for one hour before serving.

Instructions:

1. Cook chorizo in a medium size fry pan over medium heat for 20 minutes or until crust starts to form on top. Let stand for 5 minutes.
2. Place about a teaspoon of chorizo into the center of each wonton wrapper then top with ¼ teaspoon of parmesan cheese. Repeat until all wontons are filled
3. Turn the filled wonton wrappers so it looks like a diamond shape then wet one side of the diamond with a little water. From here fold the other side of the dry side of the diamond over to form a triangle marking sure the edges are formed together and closed completely. Repeat process until all the wontons wrappers are fold over and closed.
4. Heat 2 ½ Tablespoons of oil in a medium fry pan over medium-high heat. Cook filled wontons on each side for about 3 minutes or until golden brown. Repeat until all are cooked. Serve with avocado ranch dip.

Stuffed Clams – Makes 4-6 clams

- 1 can minced clams
- 1 teaspoon bottled minced garlic
- 1 teaspoon fine diced yellow onion
- 1 teaspoon fine diced red bell pepper
- ¼ teaspoon bottled lemon juice
- ¼ teaspoon green hot sauce
- ¼ teaspoon Worcestershire sauce
- 1 egg
- 2 ½ Tablespoons plain bread crumbs
- 2 Tablespoons melted margarine
- 4-6 Saved Clam Shells

Instructions:

1. Preheat oven on 325 degrees. Stir together the first seven ingredients in a mixing bowl then fold in the egg and bread crumbs into the mixture.
2. Spoon about a tablespoon of clam mixture into each of the empty saved clam shells and once all the mixture is spooned into the shells then brush each with melted margarine. *This will help get a nice golden brown color on top.*
3. Place stuffed clam shells on a medium baking pan bake for 10 minutes then remove from oven and serve.

Tuna Wontons – Makes 16 wontons

- **16 wonton wrappers**
- **1 (4.5ounce) package hickory smoked tuna**
- **1 ¼ Tablespoons can petite diced tomatoes**
- **3 Tablespoons mayo**
- **dashes ground black pepper**
- **dashes paprika**
- **1 lemon sauce recipe (see page 180)**

Instructions:

1. In a small bowl mix tuna with mayo and season with ground black pepper and paprika stirring everything together. Preheat oven on 325 degrees.
2. Turn wonton wrapper so it looks like a diamond then place in the middle 1 ½ teaspoons of tuna mixture then with water wet the four corners then fold one side over the mixture making sure to press down and close the wonton. The finished filled wonton should look like a triangle with the edge sealed closed. Repeat with remaining wontons until all are filled.
3. Place on a large greased baking pan bake for 15-20 minutes. Remove from oven and serve with lemon sauce.

Crab & Andouille Sausage Wontons – Makes 26 wontons

- 1 (6ounce) can fancy white crab meat (drained)
- 1 fully cooked andouille sausage
- 1 ½ Tablespoons diced yellow onion
- 1 ½ Tablespoons diced red bell pepper
- ¼ cup bag baby spinach
- ½ teaspoon bottled minced garlic
- 1 ½ Tablespoons bottled shrimp scampi sauce
- 1 Tablespoon margarine
- 26 wonton wrappers

Make Ahead

Remove stems from baby spinach rinse then chop and set aside until needed. Dice the andouille sausage and set aside.

Instructions:

1. In a medium non-stick pan cook onion, pepper, garlic and andouille over medium heat for 5 minutes. Add crab, sauce and spinach to pan stirring everything together let cook for 1-2 minutes.
2. Preheat oven on 350 degrees then start assembling wontons. Turn wonton wrapper so it looks like a diamond then place in the middle 1 teaspoons of crab mixture then with water wet the four corners then fold one side over the mixture making sure to press down and close the wonton. The finished filled wonton should look like a triangle with the edge sealed closed. Repeat with remaining wontons until all are filled. Using the back edges of a fork can help seal the wonton if needed.
3. Melt margarine in microwave then evenly baste each finished wonton with melted margarine place wontons on a large pizza pan sprayed with no-stick place in oven to bake for 10 minutes or until tops start to brown. Remove from heat and serve.

Mini Calzones – Makes 10 calzones

- **3 Tablespoons can chopped black olives**
- **2 ½ Tablespoons fine diced yellow onion**
- **¼ cup bag shredded Colby & jack**
- **2 teaspoons margarine**
- **¼ teaspoon garlic powder**
- **jar pizza sauce**
- **10 wonton wrappers**

Tip

    Any toppings can be used when making mini calzones such pepperoni, ham, pineapple, or mushrooms to name a few try different combinations.

Instructions:

1. Mix black olives and diced onion together set aside. Preheat oven on 350 degrees then start assembling calzones.
2. Turn wonton wrapper so it looks like a diamond then place in the middle of each wonton 1 teaspoon of black olive mixture evenly top each with cheese. Using a very small amount of water wet the four corners then fold one side over the mixture making sure to press down and close the wonton. The finished filled wonton should look like a triangle with the edge sealed closed. Use the back tip of a fork to help seal wontons by pressing down around the edge of the finished triangle.
3. Place finished wontons on a medium pizza pan sprayed with no-stick. Melt margarine in microwave then whisk in garlic powder. Baste each finished wonton with garlic butter then place in oven to bake for 10-15 minutes or until they start to brown. Remove from oven and serve with a bowl of pizza sauce.

Tuna Cake Sliders – Makes 6 sliders

- **1 (4.5ounce) package hickory smoked tuna**
- **2 Tablespoons diced yellow onion**
- **2 Tablespoons diced red bell pepper**
- **1 ½ Tablespoons light mayo**
- **¼ teaspoon bottled lemon juice**
- **¼ cup plain panko bread crumbs**
- **dashes paprika**
- **dashes ground black pepper**
- **dash sea salt**
- **6 dinner rolls**
- **1 medium tomato**
- **¾ cup bag baby spinach**
- **1 Tablespoon Italian dressing**

Make Ahead

Remove stems from spinach rinse then toss with Italian dressing then rinse and thinly slice tomato place spinach and sliced tomato in refrigerator until needed.

Instructions:

1. Preheat oven on 350 degrees then mix the first 9 ingredients in a medium mixing bowl. Once ingredients are throroughly mixed then spoon out 2 Tablespoons of tuna mixture and form into small cakes. Repeat with remaining tuna mixture until all 6 cakes are made.
2. Place tuna cakes on a small baking pan sprayed with no-stick and bake for 20-25 minutes or until cakes start to brown. Remove from oven then assemble sliders by cutting open a dinner roll place one cake on the bottom of the roll and top with a slice of tomato and about ounce of spinach place top part of roll on top then serve. Repeat until all sliders have been made.

Honey- Mustard Shrimp Sliders – Makes 6 sliders

- **18 extra large shrimp (rinsed removing shells including tails shells and veins)**
- **3/8 cup honey**
- **½ cup yellow mustard**
- **¾ cup bag baby spinach (rinsed stems removed)**
- **6 dinner rolls**

Make Ahead

Place shrimp into a large resealable bag then in a medium bowl whisk together mustard and honey add mixture to bag making sure to cover all shrimp. Let marinate in refrigerator for 6-8 hours.

Instructions:

1. Preheat oven on 300 degrees then place marinated shrimp on a large baking pan sprayed with no-stick and let bake for 5-7 minutes or until shrimp are opaque.
2. Remove shrimp from oven assemble sliders by cutting open the dinner rolls place 3 shrimp per roll and evenly top each with spinach then serve.

Potato Skins – Makes 8 potato skins

- **2 large Idaho® bake potatoes**
- **2 Tablespoons margarine**
- **3 teaspoons sour cream & onion seasoning**
- **¼ cup bag shredded cheddar cheese**
- **4 teaspoons bottled bacon bits**

Instructions:

1. Rinse potatoes then with a fork poke lots of holes in each potato both sides this will keep it from exploding in the microwave then microwave for 5 minute intervals on medium heat.
2. Once the potato is a little soft felling remove from microwave and let stand for 5-8 minutes or until potato is cool enough to handle.
3. Preheat oven on 325 degrees. Cut each potato in half then cut each half in half there should be 8 halves when done.
4. Using a small knife remove some of the potato pulp from each half until the pulp is flat about 1-1 ½ inch of pulp left.
5. Melt margarine in microwave once melted stir in sour cream & onion seasoning once dissolved evenly brush each potato half with margarine mixture.
6. Once that is done then place potatoes on a medium baking pan sprayed with no-stick and place in oven bake for 10 minutes. Once the 10 minutes is up then remove from oven and evenly sprinkle each potato with cheese then bacon and place back in oven continuing to bake for another 5-8 minutes or until cheese is melted. Remove from heat and serve.

Idaho® potatoes is a registered certification mark owned by the Idaho Potato Commission that certifies potatoes that are grown in the State of Idaho.

Stuffed Mushrooms – Makes 8-10 mushrooms

- **1 French roll (cubed)**
- **1 package maple sausage links**
- **¼ cup diced red bell pepper**
- **¼ cup diced yellow onion**
- **2 teaspoons bottled minced garlic**
- **1 Tablespoon butter or margarine**
- **1 egg**
- **2 teaspoons grated parmesan**
- **1 teaspoon ground black pepper**
- **¾ cup low-sodium chicken broth**
- **8-10 large button mushrooms**

Instructions:

1. In a medium fry pan cook sausage links over medium heat for 10-15 minutes or until cooked all the way through turning once halfway through. Once cooked set aside to let cool then dice the sausage up.
2. Preheat oven on 325 degrees place cubed French roll on a greased pan and place in oven for about 5-7 minutes or until bread is firm and toasted.
3. In a large mixing bowl place the toasted cubed bread and grated parmesan. Preheat oven to 375 degrees.
4. Rinse mushrooms and remove the stems then set inside part down on paper towels to help drain any water off the mushrooms while the stuffing gets made.
5. In a medium fry pan sauté bell pepper, onion, and garlic in butter or margarine over medium heat for about 5 minutes or until veggies are tender.
6. Add the sautéed veggies, sausage, chicken broth, ground black pepper, and egg to the bread and parmesan mixture and toss together. The egg will act as a binder to hold everything together.
7. Spoon about a teaspoon amount of stuffing mixture into each mushroom and place stuffed mushrooms on a medium baking pan sprayed with no-stick and place in oven to bake for 25-30 minutes until the top is golden brown then serve.

Crab Stuffed Mushrooms – Makes 13 mushrooms

- 1 (6ounce) can lump crab meat (drained)
- 1 egg
- ¼ teaspoon salt
- 2 teaspoons diced yellow onion
- 2 teaspoons diced red bell pepper
- 1 teaspoon bottled lemon juice
- dashes ground red pepper
- ½ teaspoon Worcestershire sauce
- 1 ½ teaspoon Dijon mustard
- 3 Tablespoons plain bread crumbs
- 1 Tablespoon dry white cooking wine
- 13 large button mushrooms

Instructions:

1. Pull stems out of mushrooms make a hole for the stuffing then rinse mushrooms and let dry stem side down on paper towel.
2. In a medium mixing bowl stir together salt, onion, bell pepper, lemon juice, ground red pepper, Worcestershire, and Dijon mustard.
3. Slowly fold in crab meat into mixture then slowly stir in the egg as well. This will help bind the mixture together.
4. Slowly fold the bread crumbs to the mixture and repeat until all the bread crumbs are in the mixture. Brush mushrooms tops with white wine then preheat oven on 325 degrees.
5. Stuff each mushroom with about 1 tablespoon of crab mixture repeat until all mushrooms are stuffed.
6. Place mushroom on a large baking pan sprayed with no-stick and place in oven bake for 25-30 minutes or until crab mixture is brown on top then remove from oven and serve.

BBQ Chicken Quesadilla – Makes 1 quesadilla

- **3 ounces cooked BBQ chicken (diced)**
- **1 Tablespoon diced yellow onion**
- **1 teaspoon can chopped black olives**
- **1 teaspoon diced red bell pepper**
- **2 Tablespoons bottled BBQ sauce**
- **¼ cup shredded Queso mixture bag cheese**
- **2 soft taco size tortillas**

Instructions:

1. Preheat oven on 375 degrees and grease a small pizza pan.
2. Take one of the tortillas sprinkle the cooked BBQ chicken on first then sprinkle the onions, olives, and bell pepper.
3. Sprinkle the cheese on last making sure to cover the other ingredients then drizzle BBQ sauce over the other ingredients making sure to cover all areas.
4. Top with the second tortilla then transfer to pizza pan. Bake for 5-6 minutes turning once halfway through. Remove from oven slice into wedges and serve.

Quesadilla with Black Bean Relish – Makes 1 quesadilla

- **2 taco size tortillas**
- **1/3 cup shredded Colby jack bag cheese**
- **½ teaspoon chili powder**

Black Bean Relish:
- **1 Tablespoon diced yellow onion**
- **1 Tablespoon diced red bell pepper**
- **3 Tablespoons can black beans**
- **2 Tablespoons can corn (drained)**
- **1 Tablespoon bottled lime juice**

Instructions:

1. In a small sauce pot mix together black bean relish ingredients and cook over very low heat uncovered for 15 minutes then remove from heat a set aside.
2. Preheat oven on 375 degrees the assemble quesadilla by taking one tortilla place cheese evenly over tortilla. Sprinkle the chili powered over the cheese evenly then top with second tortilla place finished quesadilla in a greased small pizza pan and bake for 5 minutes turning over once halfway through.
3. Remove from oven then cut into wedges and serve with black bean relish.

Crab Rolls – Makes 5 rolls

- **1 (6ounce) can crab meat lump (drained)**
- **2 ½ Tablespoons diced yellow onion**
- **2 Tablespoons diced red bell pepper**
- **½ cup shredded lettuce**
- **½ teaspoon bottle minced garlic**
- **1 teaspoon lemon-pepper seasoning**
- **5 egg roll wrappers**
- **2 ½ Tablespoons butter or margarine**

Instructions:

1. Melt 1 Tablespoon butter over medium-low heat in a medium skillet then add diced onion, diced bell pepper, and garlic sauté for 2 minutes.
2. Add drained crab meat and lemon pepper seasoning to pan stirring everything together and cook for another 1-2 minutes then remove from heat.
3. Melt 1 ½ Tablespoons of butter in the microwave and preheat oven on 375 degrees.
4. Start to assemble rolls by having wrapper turned so it looks like a diamond then place 2 Tablespoons of crab meat mixture towards the bottom corner then top with some lettuce.
5. Roll corner over mixture once tightly then fold in both side and continue rolling wet the last corner with a little water to help the wrapper stick then finish rolling repeat with remaining wrappers.
6. Place finished crab stuffed rolls on a small pizza pan sprayed with no-stick then brush the top of each roll with the some melted butter. Place in oven and bake for 15 minutes or until the tops start to brown remove from oven and serve.

Shrimp Egg Rolls – Makes 6 rolls

- ¼ pound raw jumbo shrimp
- 1 diced fully-cooked andouille sausage
- 3 Tablespoons diced yellow onion
- 2 ½ Tablespoons diced red bell pepper
- 1 teaspoon bottled minced garlic
- ½ Tablespoon chili powder
- ¾ cup bag spinach leaves
- ¼ cup Italian dressing
- 2 Tablespoons olive oil
- 1 Tablespoon melted butter or margarine
- 6 egg roll wrappers

Instructions:

* Make ahead*

Rinse shrimp (removing shells including tails shells and devein if needed). In a small plastic sandwich bag marinate shrimp with Italian dressing for 4 hours and once shrimp are done marinating chop up shrimp into small pieces.

1. In a medium skillet heat olive oil over medium-low heat then add the diced andouille sausage, diced onion, diced bell pepper, and minced garlic sauté for a second then add the chili powder making sure to stir everything together.
2. Cook for 2-3 minutes continually stirring around so garlic does not burn then add diced shrimp continue to cook for 1 minute then lower heat and cover and let cook for another minute or until shrimp is opaque then remove from heat.
3. Preheat oven on 375 degrees then start to assemble the rolls by having wrapper turned so it looks like a diamond then place 3 Tablespoons of shrimp mixture towards the bottom corner then top with some spinach leaves.
4. Roll corner over mixture once tightly then fold in both side and continue rolling wet the last corner with a little water to help the wrapper stick then finish rolling repeat with remaining wrappers.
5. Place finished shrimp stuffed rolls on a small pizza pan sprayed with no-stick then brush the top of each roll with the melted butter. Place in oven and bake for 15 minutes or until tops start to brown remove from oven and serve.

Southwestern Egg Rolls – Makes 8-10 rolls

- ¾ pound chicken breast tenderloins
- ½ teaspoon fajita seasoning
- 3 Tablespoons diced yellow onion
- 3 Tablespoons diced red bell pepper
- 2 Tablespoons can corn (drained)
- ¼ cup can black beans (drained)
- 1 teaspoon bottled minced garlic
- ½ teaspoon chili powder
- 1 teaspoon bottled lime juice
- ½ cup bag spinach leaves
- 2 Tablespoons olive oil
- 1 Tablespoons melted butter or margarine
- 8-10 egg roll wrappers

Instructions:

* Make ahead*

    Rinse chicken then sprinkle chicken breast tenderloins both sides evenly with ½ teaspoon of fajita seasoning and place in plastic bag and marinate overnight in refrigerator.

1. Heat a non-stick pan over medium-heat and add seasoned chicken breast tenderloins. Cook for 10-12 minutes turning once half way through.
2. Remove from heat let cool for 5 minutes or until cool enough to handle then dice up chicken and set aside. Remove stems for spinach then rinse and set aside.
3. Heat oil over medium-low heat in a medium pan then add onion, bell pepper, black beans, corn, minced garlic, lime juice, and chili powder cook for 1-2 minutes continually stirring
4. Add chicken to mixture in the pan and cook for another 1-2 minutes continually stirring then remove from heat and let cool enough to be handled.
5. Preheat oven on 375 degrees then start to assemble the rolls

by having wrapper turned so it looks like a diamond then place 2 Tablespoons of chicken mixture towards the bottom corner then top with some spinach leaves.

6. Roll corner over mixture once tightly then fold in both sides and continue rolling wet the last corner with a little water to help the wrapper stick then finish rolling repeat with remaining wrappers.

7. Place finished chicken stuffed rolls on a medium pizza pan sprayed with no-stick then brush the top of each roll with the melted butter. Place in oven and bake for 15 minutes or until tops start to brown remove from oven and can be served with salsa, sour cream, or guacamole.

Chicken Potstickers – Makes 19 potstickers

- **1 boneless skinless chicken breast (rinse chicken)**
- **4 whole white button mushrooms**
- **¾ cup bag baby spinach**
- **3 Tablespoons bottled garlic teriyaki sauce**
- **½ teaspoon bottled minced garlic**
- **3 Tablespoons diced yellow onion**
- **1 teaspoon dry cooking white wine**
- **1 teaspoon margarine**
- **1 teaspoon bottled lemon juice**
- **1 cup low-sodium chicken broth**
- **dashes salt**
- **dashes ground black pepper**
- **19 wonton skins**

Instructions:

1. Preheat oven to 325 degrees then baste chicken with 2 tablespoons of teriyaki sauce both sides and place in oven to bake for 30 minutes or until chicken is not pink inside.
2. Remove stems from mushrooms then rinse set on paper towel to dry. Remove stems from baby spinach then rinse and set aside.
3. Dice mushrooms caps and do a rough chop of the baby spinach then place in refrigerator.
4. Once chicken is done let cool for 5 minutes or until cool enough to handle then dice up chicken and set aside.
5. In a medium skillet melt margarine over medium-high heat then add diced mushrooms, diced onion, and minced garlic season with salt and pepper. Cook mushroom mixture for 2-3 minutes stirring occasionally then add white wine, lemon juice, and spinach to pan stirring everything together.
6. Continue to cook for 1-2 more minutes stirring occasionally then stir chicken into pan mixing everything together.
7. Start to assemble the potstickers by having wrapper turned

so it looks like a diamond then place 1-1 ½ teaspoons of chicken mixture in the middle moist the top corner with a little water which will help seal the wonton.

8. Fold over the bottom corner over the mixture sealing with the top corner make sure to press so the wonton seals. Use the back edge of a fork on the edges of the wonton to help seal. Repeat with remaining wontons keep wontons on plate cover with a damp cloth to keep them from drying out.

9. In a large pan heat about ¼ cup of chicken broth make sure it is enough to cover the bottom of the pan then add the finished wontons about 6-8 at a time cover and steam for 5-6 minutes remove from pan set aside.

10. Add ¼ cup more of broth to pan then add another batch of wontons cover and steam for 5-6 minutes. Repeat this process until all wontons are cooked and continue to add chicken broth as needed. Once all wontons are cooked serve them alone or with soy or Chinese mustard

Grilled Buffalo Wings – Makes 2-4 servings

- **1 pound fresh chicken wings (rinse chicken)**
- **½ cup wing sauce with additional 3 oz set aside**

Tip

This is a spicy dish. By adding small amounts of melted butter or margarine to wing sauce can help take away some of the heat of the sauce.

Instructions:

1. Rinse chicken in cold water then discard the wing tips. Preheat grill.
2. Take 3 oz of wing sauce and brush on each chicken wing (skin-side) set aside
3. Grill wings on direct heat the skin side down first for about 20 minutes then 5 minutes before turning over brush each wing with wing sauce (meat side)
4. Turn wings over (meat side down) cook for about 25-30 minutes or until juices run clear. Let set for 5 minutes before serving.

Grilled Italian Wings – Makes 2-4 servings

- **1 ¾ pound fresh chicken wings**
- **1 cup Italian dressing (¼ cup set aside)**

Make Ahead

Rinse chicken in cold water then discard the wing tips put wings in large bag with ¾ cup Italian dressing and put in refrigerator to marinate overnight.

Instructions:

1. Preheat grill. Grill wings on direct heat the skin side down first for about 20 minutes then 5 minutes before turning over brush each wing with Italian dressing (meat side).
2. Turn wings over (meat side down) cook for about 25-30 minutes or until juices run clear and the last 10 minutes brush the remaining Italian dressing on the up facing side (skin-side). Let set for 5 minutes before serving.

Lemon-Pepper Wings – Makes 2-4 servings

- **14 raw chicken wings**
- **1 ¼ Tablespoon lemon pepper seasoning**
- **lemon sauce recipe (see page 180)**

Make Ahead

Rinse chicken in cold water then discard the wing tips and make the lemon sauce cover keep warm on low heat.

Instructions:

1. Preheat oven on 350 degrees then evenly season each chicken wing both sides with lemon-pepper seasoning. Place seasoned wings on a large baking pan sprayed with no-stick and bake for 50-55 minutes or until juices run clear. The last 15 minutes turn heat up to 375 degrees.
2. Once wings are cooked then toss in lemon sauce and serve.

Buffalo Nuggets – Makes 4-6 servings

- **2 boneless skinless chicken breast (rinse chicken)**
- **2/3 cups plain bread crumbs**
- **1/3 cup milk**
- **1 egg**
- **¼ - 1/3 cup buffalo wing sauce**

Tip

This is a spicy dish. By adding small amounts of melted butter or margarine to wing sauce can help take away some of the heat of the sauce.

Instructions:

1. Pre heat oven on 350 degrees. Cut chicken into cubes about ½ inch to inch in size then set aside. In shallow bowl whisk together milk with the egg and in another shallow bowl add the bread crumbs.
2. Dip the cubes of chicken into the milk mixture coating both sides and shake off any excess then dredge through the bread crumbs being sure to coat all sides. Repeat with remaining chicken cubes. Place coated chicken cubes on a medium baking pan sprayed with no-stick.
3. Place baking pan with coated chicken in oven for 25-30 minutes or until no longer pink in the middle turning once halfway through to make sure both sides brown.
4. Remove from heat once cooked let sit. In the microwave warm up the wing sauce then in a large bowl toss the cooked chicken cubes with the wing sauce making sure to cover nuggets completely and serve with ranch or bleu cheese dressing.

Section 2

Breakfast

Quick Biscuits & Gravy – Makes 5 biscuits

- **1 tube of buttermilk biscuits**
- **1 sausage country gravy recipe (see page 186)**

Instructions:

1. Preheat oven at 325 degrees then place biscuits on pan then place in oven.
2. After about 5-6 minutes check biscuits to see if bottom is done then flip over all biscuits to cook the other side for another 5 minutes. (***This helps keep the biscuits from getting to hard***)
3. Once biscuits are done serve with sausage country gravy.

Egg & Avocado Sandwich – Makes 4 sandwiches

- **4 eggs**
- **2 teaspoons milk**
- **1 avocado sliced**
- **¼ cup bag shredded Colby & jack cheese**
- **dashes green hot sauce**
- **dashes ground black pepper**
- **4 French rolls**

Instructions:

1. In a small bowl whisk eggs, milk, and green hot sauce together. Heat medium non-stick pan sprayed with no-stick over medium-low heat and scrambles the egg mixture until no longer runny or cook all the way through.
2. While eggs are cooking, set oven on low broil place cheese on each French roll and place under broiler until cheese melts. Once the eggs are done and rolls ready it is time to assemble the sandwiches.
3. Add some ground black pepper to eggs and spoon eggs between each roll and add sliced avocado to each roll then serve.

Egg Bagel Sandwich – Makes 4 sandwiches

- **8 eggs (whites only)**
- **2 (6ounce) fully cooked ham steaks**
- **2 ½ Tablespoons Dijon mustard**
- **2 Tablespoons honey**
- **4 slices white American cheese**
- **4 bagels**
- **dashes ground black pepper**
- **dashes paprika**

Instructions:

1. Whisk together Dijon and honey then baste ham steaks both sides set aside. Heat a large non-stick pan over medium heat and add the ham steaks. Cook for 6-8 minutes turning once halfway through then remove from heat set aside.
2. Heat a large non-stick pan over medium-low heat. Then add the egg whites cover pan let cook for 5-6 minutes or until eggs are no longer runny. The last 1-2 minutes season eggs with ground pepper and paprika. Top eggs with cheese return cover and turn burner off; let cheese melt.
3. Once cheese is melted then assemble sandwiches by cutting the ham steaks in half then place a piece of ham steak on bottom part of each bagel then evenly top each with eggs there should be two eggs per sandwich add top part of bagel then serve.

Deviled Eggs – Makes 6 eggs

- **3 large hard boiled eggs**
- **1 ½ Tablespoon mayo**
- **1 ½ teaspoon of Dijon mustard**
- **dashes garlic powder**
- **dashes onion powder**
- **dashes paprika**
- **dashes ground black pepper**

Instructions:

1. Split each hard boiled egg in half lengthwise around the eggs to expose the yolk. Take each yolk out of each egg and put into a small bowl. Mash the yolk lightly with a fork
2. Add the mayo, ground black pepper, and mustard to mashed yolks and work into the yolk with the fork.
3. Once all ingredients are mixed together then spoon about ¼ teaspoon into the center of each egg and once all eggs are filled sprinkle each with paprika then chill before serving.

French Toast with a Banana Twist – Makes 4-6 French toast

- 2 eggs (beaten)
- ½ cup milk
- 1 Tablespoon sugar
- 1 teaspoon vanilla
- 1 teaspoon cinnamon
- 1 teaspoon banana flavored liqueur
- 4-6 slices sourdough bread

Instructions:

1. Preheat griddle on medium-low heat.
2. In a medium bowl whisk all ingredients together then pour into a shallow bowl.
3. Dip each piece of bread into mixture coating both sides then place on heated griddle.
4. Cook on each side for about 5 minutes or until golden brown then serve.

Apple & Cinnamon Pancakes – Makes 8-10 pancakes

- **1 cup quick biscuit mix**
- **2/3 cup milk**
- **1 egg**
- **1 green apple (diced)**
- **1 Tablespoon sugar**
- **1 Tablespoon margarine**
- **2 Tablespoons cinnamon/sugar mixture**

Tip

I make the cinnamon/sugar mixture ahead of time and store. It is equal parts cinnamon and sugar such as ½ cup cinnamon and ½ cup sugar mixed together.

Instructions:

1. Heat medium fry pan over medium-low heat and melt margarine then add the diced apple and 2 Tablespoons of cinnamon sugar mixture and stir together. Cook for about 6-10 minutes or until apple is tender.
2. Preheat griddle on medium-low heat. In a large mixing bowl combine biscuit mix, milk, egg, and sugar. Mix well until a smooth pancake batter is made. Fold apple mixture to pancake batter.
3. Pour about ¼ cup of batter onto heated griddle and cook for about 5 minutes or until golden brown then flip and repeat on other side. Repeat with the remaining batter mix and then serve.

Cranberry & Orange Pancakes – Makes 8-10 pancakes

- **1 cup quick biscuit mix**
- **2/3 cups milk**
- **1 egg**
- **2 Tablespoons sugar**
- **2/3 cups whole fresh cranberries**
- **1 ½ teaspoon orange extract**

Make Ahead

Rinse cranberries then dice and place in a container with 1 Tablespoon of sugar stirring together then place in refrigerator for 2-3 hours.

Instructions:

1. Preheat griddle on medium-low heat. In a large mixing bowl combine biscuit mix, milk, egg, and sugar. Mix well until a smooth pancake batter is made. Stir in cranberries and orange extract.
2. Pour about ¼ cup of batter onto heated griddle and cook for about 5 minutes or until golden brown then flip and repeat on other side. Repeat with the remaining batter mix and then serve.

Huevos Rancheros – Makes 4 servings

- **8 eggs**
- **¼ cup milk**
- **2 teaspoon chili powder**
- **1/3 cup diced yellow onion**
- **1/3 cup diced red bell pepper**
- **2 Tablespoon butter or margarine**
- **¾ cup can green enchilada sauce**
- **dashes salt**
- **3 Tablespoons bag shredded Queso blend cheese**
- **4 taco size tortillas**

Instructions:

1. In a medium skillet melt butter over medium-low heat then add onion and bell pepper season with salt; cook for 1-2 minutes stirring occasionally.
2. Whisk together eggs and milk in mixing bowl then add beaten egg mixture to pan with onion and bell pepper mixture continually stirring around in order to scramble eggs.
3. Once eggs are done which they will be cooked but still light and fluffy add the chili powder mixing into the egg mixture then add enchilada sauce turn heat down to low and cover. Cook for 5 minutes then remove from heat. Spoon mixture onto plates top with cheese and serve with warm tortillas.

Egg Quesadilla – Makes 4 servings

- **4 eggs**
- **2 taco size tortillas**
- **1/3 cup shredded Colby jack bag cheese**
- **½ teaspoon chili powder**
- **2 Tablespoons can black beans**
- **½ cup can green enchilada sauce**

Make Ahead

Evenly sprinkle the cheese, chili powder, and black beans on one tortilla top with the other tortilla and place in refrigerator until ready to make.

Instructions:

1. Using an egg poacher pan fill with ½ inch water then spray poaching cups with non-stick place cups back in poaching pan. Turn heat up to medium then cover pan let poacher warm up. Once the water starts to simmer add eggs into poaching cups return cover. Let the eggs cook for 5-8 minutes or until completely cooked or until preferred doneness.
2. Once eggs have started to cook then place quesadilla on a medium baking pan sprayed with no-stick in a preheated oven on 350 degrees and bake for 5 minutes. Place enchilada sauce in a microwavable dish and warm up in microwave.
3. Once eggs, enchilada sauce, and quesadilla are done it is time to start assembling the dish. Cut quesadilla into quarters. Place each piece of quesadilla on a plate top each with a poached egg then evenly top each egg with enchilada sauce and serve.

Twist on Eggs Benedict – Makes 4-8 servings

- **8 eggs**
- **8 slices peppered bacon**
- **8 slices provolone**
- **1 large tomato (rinsed & thinly sliced)**
- **1 package hollandaise sauce**
- **4 English muffins**
- **dashes paprika**

Make Ahead

Follow directions on package and cook bacon then set aside until needed. Next, follow the directions on the hollandaise sauce package and make sauce. Once sauce is made keep covered on very low heat while making the eggs. Stir the sauce before putting on top of poached eggs in the last step.

Instructions:

1. Using an egg poacher pan fill with ½ inch water then spray poaching cups with non-stick place cups back in poaching pan. Turn heat up to medium then cover pan let poacher warm up. Once the water starts to simmer add eggs into poaching cups return cover. Let the eggs cook for 5-8 minutes or until completely cooked or until preferred doneness. Repeat with remaining eggs.
2. The last few minutes of eggs cooking heat oven on 400 degrees then slice English muffins in half and cut strips in half then put bacon on top of muffins 2 halves per muffin top each with a slice of provolone. Place muffins on a large baking pan sprayed with no-stick and let bake for 1-2 minutes or until cheese is melted.
3. Remove muffins from oven and plate by placing a thinly slice of tomato on each then one poached egg on top of each muffin. Evenly spoon hollandaise sauce over each egg and sprinkle each with paprika and serve.

Hash Brown – Makes 4 servings

- **3 Idaho® potatoes peeled**
- **3 Tablespoons sour cream & onion seasoning**
- **3 Tablespoons cheddar cheese seasoning**
- **3 Tablespoons margarine**
- **dashes salt**
- **dashes ground black pepper**

Instructions:

1. Rinse potatoes then using a grater shredded potatoes.
2. In a large pan over medium heat melt margarine then add shredded potatoes to pan seasoning with salt and pepper.
3. Add the sour cream & onion and cheddar cheese seasoning to potatoes stirring around cook potatoes for 5-7 minutes on once side once potatoes start to brown turn them over.
4. Cook on other side for another 5-7 or until bottom browns once both sides of potatoes are brown remove from heat and serve.

Section 3

Sandwiches
&
Salads

Sandwiches

Easy Sloppy Joes – Makes 4 sandwiches

- **1 pound ground beef**
- **1 Tablespoon Worcestershire sauce**
- **1 teaspoon brown sugar**
- **1 Tablespoon yellow mustard**
- **1 teaspoon mesquite liquid smoke**
- **1 ½ cups tomato, garlic, & onion tomato sauce**
- **dashes salt**
- **dashes ground black pepper**
- **dashes green hot sauce**
- **4 hamburger rolls**

Instructions:

1. In a large skillet add ground beef cook for 10-15 minutes over medium heat or until beef is brown and cooked through. Drain any fat from pan then add the Worcestershire sauce and brown sugar stirring everything together cook for another minute.
2. Add mustard, tomato sauce, liquid smoke, salt, pepper, and hot sauce to beef then stir everything together. Bring mixture to boil then turn heat down and let simmer for 5 minutes stirring frequently Remove from heat evenly spoon beef mixture onto hamburger rolls and serve.

Meatball Sandwiches – Makes 5 sandwiches

- ¾ pound ground beef
- 1 ½ Tablespoons prime rib seasoning
- 1 (8ounce) can plain tomato sauce
- ¼ cup grated parmesan
- 3 Tablespoons garlic powder
- 3 Tablespoons onion powder
- 10 slices provolone
- 5 French rolls

Instructions:

1. In bowl mix beef with prime rib seasoning then form meatballs about the size of a golf ball and should get about 10 meatballs.
2. Heat large fry pan sprayed with no-stick add meatballs cook for about 3 minutes over medium heat turning once and once brown on outside. Lower heat to medium-low heat cover and cook for 10-15 minutes until no pink inside.
3. While meatballs are cooking; in a large sauce pot add tomato sauce, grated parmesan, garlic powder, and onion powder stir together. Let tomato sauce cook over medium-low heat for 10 minutes.
4. Once meatballs are cooked add to tomato sauce. Turn heat down to low cover and simmer for 15 minutes. Place 2 slices of provolone on each roll then add 2 meatballs to each roll spoon any left over sauce on sandwiches then serve.

Italian Steak Sandwiches – Makes 4-6 sandwiches

- 1 ¼ pound chuck steak thin cut
- 1 cup sliced yellow onion
- ½ cup strips red bell pepper
- ¾ cup Italian herb dressing
- 4 teaspoons of margarine or butter
- dashes salt
- dashes ground black pepper
- 4-6 slices provolone cheese
- 4-6 French rolls

Tip

The steak will be rare cook longer for more well done steak.

Make Ahead

Marinate steak in Italian herb dressing overnight in refrigerator.

Instructions:

1. Heat grill on medium-high heat. Drain marinates cook steak over direct heat for 5-10 minutes turning only once halfway through. Once steak is cooked let rest for 5 minutes.
2. Melt margarine or butter in a large skillet on the stove over medium heat then add onions and bell pepper season with salt and ground black pepper.
3. Sauté onion and bell pepper mixture for 5-8 minutes. Meanwhile, thinly slice the steak into strips then add to onion pepper mixture tossing everything together and cook for 1 minute.
4. Place a slice of provolone cheese on French roll then top with some of the steak, onion, and bell pepper mixture then serve.

Fish Sandwich – Makes 4 sandwiches

- **¾ -1 pound cod fillets**
- **1 ½ Tablespoons lemon-pepper seasoning**
- **3 ounces all-purpose flour**
- **1 ¼ cup oil**
- **1 sliced tomato**
- **lettuce**
- **tarter sauce or mayo**
- **4 Onion rolls**

Instructions:

1. Cut cod fillet into 4 pieces and heat oil in large skillet over medium-low heat.
2. Take 2 ½ teaspoons of lemon pepper seasoning and season all four pieces of the cod evenly on both sides. Take the remaining 1 ½ teaspoons of lemon pepper seasoning and mix with the flour.
3. Once oil is heated coat the cod fillets both sides with the seasoned flour then add to pan. Cook for 6-8 minutes on each side or until fish is cook all the way through.
4. Drain fish on a plate with a paper towel before assembling sandwiches.
5. Spread a thin layer of tarter sauce or mayo on top part of bun then on the bottom part of the bun place the fish and top with some lettuce and tomato then add the top part of the bun and serve.

Cajun Tilapia Wraps – Makes 4 Wraps

- **4 tilapia fillets**
- **3 ½ teaspoons Cajun seasoning**
- **¾ cup shredded lettuce**
- **1 large tomato (sliced)**
- **1 avocado (sliced)**
- **4 soft taco size tortillas**

Tip

> **This is a spicy dish.**

Instructions:

1. Preheat oven on 325 degrees. Evenly season each piece of tilapia with Cajun seasoning on both sides. Place on a large non-stick baking pan bake for 35 minutes or until cooked through
2. Rinse tomato then thinly slice and slice avocado. Once tilapia is done remove from oven place the four tilapia fillets in the middle of each tortilla then evenly top each with lettuce, tomato, and avocado then wrap and serve.

Buffalo Shrimp Sandwich – Makes 4 sandwiches

- **24 extra large raw shrimp**
- **¼ cup buffalo wing sauce**
- **1 cup shredded lettuce**
- **½ cup thinly sliced yellow onion**
- **¼ cup crumbled bleu cheese**
- **4 onion hamburger rolls**

Tip

This is a spicy dish. By adding small amounts of melted butter or margarine to wing sauce can help take away some of the heat of the sauce.

Instructions:

1. Rinse, devein, remove shells, and tails of shrimp. In a small pot heat buffalo wing sauce over low heat.
2. Heat a large non-stick pan over medium-low heat cook shrimp for 5-7 minutes turning once halfway through and cook until shrimp turns opaque.
3. Once shrimp are cooked toss shrimp in wing sauce covering all shrimp then place about 6 shrimp on each roll then evenly top with bleu cheese, onion, and lettuce and serve.

Crab Cake Sandwiches - Makes 4 sandwiches

- **1 can lump crab meat (drained)**
- **1 egg**
- **¼ teaspoon salt**
- **2 teaspoons fine diced yellow onion**
- **2 teaspoons fine diced red bell pepper**
- **1 teaspoon bottled lemon juice**
- **dashes ground red pepper**
- **½ teaspoon Worcestershire sauce**
- **½ teaspoon dry mustard**
- **1/3 cup dry bread crumbs (2 tablespoons extra set aside on a plate)**
- **2 Tablespoons butter**
- **4 hamburger rolls**
- **1 avocado salsa recipe (see page 188)**

Tip

Make the avocado salsa ahead of time and let chill for 2 hours before using.

Instructions:

1. In a medium mixing bowl stir together salt, onion, bell pepper, lemon juice, ground red pepper, Worcestershire, and dry mustard.
2. Slowly fold crab meat into mixture then slowly stir in the egg as well which will help bind the mixture together. Slowly fold the bread crumbs into the crab mixture.
3. Make four balls out of mixture then press to form cakes. Heat 2 tablespoons of butter in a cast iron skillet over medium heat.
4. Take formed cakes and dredge in the extra tablespoons of bread crumbs that where set aside earlier. Once all four cakes have been dredge through the extra bread crumbs then add to hot skillet.
5. Cook for about 2-3 minutes on each side or until they are golden brown. Remove from heat then assemble sandwiches. Place once crab cake on each bottom part of the buns then evenly top each with avocado salsa add top part of bun and serve.

Grinder Sandwiches – Makes 4 sandwiches

- **12 slices hard salami**
- **8 slices pepperoni**
- **8 slices honey ham**
- **2 ½ Tablespoons finely diced medium sweet onion**
- **2 ½ Tablespoons finely diced red bell pepper**
- **4 slices provolone cheese**
- **½ vinaigrette recipe (see page 187)**
- **4 French rolls**

Instructions:

1. Preheat grill then cut each provolone cheese slice in half and mix diced onion and bell pepper together and set all aside.
2. Make vinaigrette and set aside then assemble sandwiches. Place provolone cheese one half on each side of the French roll then layer 3 slices of hard salami, 2 slices pepperoni, 2 slices of honey ham, and top with 1 – 1 ¼ Tablespoons of onion mixture. Continue until all four sandwiches are assembled then wrap each finished sandwich in heavy duty foil.
3. Place foil wrapped sandwiches on the grill over in-direct heat and let warm up for 5-6 minutes then remove from heat. Open each sandwich then add vinaigrette and serve.

Parmesan & Pepper Chicken Tender Sandwich – Makes 4 sandwiches

- 1 parmesan & pepper chicken tender recipe (see page 108)
- 1 Dijon sauce recipe (see page 182)
- 4 slices white American cheese
- 4 hamburger rolls

Tip

Make the parmesan & pepper chicken tenders first and keep warm in oven then make the Dijon sauce keeping covered so it stays warm as well.

Instructions:

1. Toast each hamburger roll and melt cheese on top part of roll then assemble sandwiches. Place two chicken tenders on the bottom bun spoon about 1 ½ Tablespoons of Dijon sauce place top bun. Repeat with remaining sandwiches then serve.

Bleu Chicken Sandwich – Makes 4 sandwiches

- **8 fully cooked chicken tenders**
- **1 cup shredded lettuce**
- **½ cup crumbled bleu cheese**
- **4 hamburger rolls**

Instructions:

1. Warm up chicken tenders in microwave.
2. Place 2 chicken tenders on each roll bottom then top with bleu cheese then bake for 2-3 minutes on 400 degrees or until cheese starts to melt.
3. Remove from oven then evenly top each with lettuce and the roll top and serve.

BBQ Chicken Sandwiches – Makes 4 sandwiches

- **4 chicken thighs**
- **1 teaspoon paprika**
- **1 teaspoon garlic powder**
- **1 teaspoon onion powder**
- **¼ teaspoon ground black pepper**
- **¼ teaspoon ground mustard**
- **¼ teaspoon hickory smoked salt**
- **BBQ sauce recipe (see page 184)**
- **4 hamburger rolls**

Make Ahead

The BBQ sauce recipe needs to be doubled for this recipe as well as made ahead of time. Once made cover and keep warm over low heat. Mix together the paprika, garlic powder, onion powder, black pepper, ground mustard and hickory smoked salt in a small bowl to make a BBQ rub. Rinse the chicken thighs; remove skin from thighs then rub with BBQ rub let marinate in refrigerator for 4 hours.

Instructions:

1. Preheat oven on 350 degrees then place chicken thighs on a medium non-stick baking pan place in oven for 40-45 or until cooked through.
2. Once chicken is cooked remove from heat let stand for 5 minutes then remove meat from bone and cut up. Place cut up chicken in pot with BBQ sauce cover let simmer over low heat for 30 minutes. After 30 minutes, spoon BBQ chickens on hamburger rolls and serve.

Lemon Chicken Wraps – Makes 4 wraps

- **2 boneless skinless chicken breast (rinse chicken)**
- **½ cup plain bread crumbs**
- **1 egg**
- **¼ cup milk**
- **1 cup lettuce**
- **1 large tomato (sliced)**
- **dashes paprika**
- **dashes ground black pepper**
- **4 taco size tortillas**
- **½ lemon recipe (see page 180)**

Instructions:

1. Preheat oven 350 degrees then in a shallow dish whisk together the egg and milk set aside. In another shallow dish mix together the bread crumbs, paprika, and ground black pepper.
2. Dip the chicken in the milk mixture covering both sides and shaking off any excess then dredge the chicken through the bread crumb mixture coating each side.
3. Place coated chicken breast on a large non-stick baking pan and place in oven. Bake for 30 minutes or until chicken is no longer pink in the middle.
4. Once chicken is done let sit for 1-2 minutes then cut each breast in half then cut each half into thin strips.
5. Place 4-5 strips in each tortilla towards one end repeating until all 4 tortillas are filled with chicken. Evenly drizzle each chicken filled tortilla with lemon sauce then evenly top each chicken filled tortilla with tomato and lettuce. Roll up each filled tortilla cut each tortilla in half then serve.

Orange Chicken Wrap – Makes 4 wraps

- **2 boneless skinless chicken breast (rinse chicken)**
- **½ cup plain bread crumbs**
- **1 egg**
- **¼ cup milk**
- **½ cups thinly sliced yellow onion**
- **½ cups thinly sliced red bell pepper**
- **2/3 cups shredded lettuce**
- **dashes paprika**
- **dashes ground black pepper**
- **4 taco size tortillas**
- **½ orange recipe (see page 181)**

Instructions:

1. Preheat oven 350 degrees then in a shallow dish whisk together the egg and milk set aside. In another shallow dish mix together the bread crumbs, paprika, and ground black pepper.
2. Dip the chicken in the milk mixture covering both sides and shaking off any excess then dredge the chicken through the bread crumb mixture coating each side.
3. Place coated chicken breast on a large non-stick baking pan and place in oven. Bake for 30 minutes or until chicken is no longer pink in the middle
4. Once chicken is done let sit for 1-2 minutes then cut each breast in half then cut each half into thin strips.
5. Place 4-5 strips in each tortilla towards one end repeating until all 4 tortillas are filled with chicken. Evenly drizzle each chicken filled tortilla with orange sauce then evenly top each chicken filled tortilla with onion, bell pepper, and lettuce.
6. Roll up each filled tortilla cut each tortilla in half then serve.

Turkey Sandwich w/Cherry Sauce – Makes 4 sandwiches

- **16 slices honey turkey breast lunchmeat**
- **1 cup shredded lettuce**
- **4 French rolls**
- **1 cherry sauce recipe (see page 190)**

Instructions:

1. Place 4 slices of turkey in each roll then evenly top each with some of the cherry sauce and top each with ¼ cup shredded lettuce and serve.

Honey-Mustard Turkey Sandwiches – Makes 4 sandwiches

- **4 turkey cutlets**
- **2 cups can fried onions**
- **2 Tablespoons honey**
- **¼ cup yellow mustard**
- **4 large hamburger rolls**
- **1 tomato (sliced)**
- **1 cup shredded lettuce**

Instructions:

1. Preheat oven on 350 degrees then in a small bowl whisk together the honey and mustard and set aside. Crush up the onions then take the turkey cutlets evenly baste with honey-mustard sauce and evenly roll each cutlet in onions covering both sides.
2. Place finished cutlets on a large baking pan sprayed with no-stick and bake for 30 minutes or until turkey is cooked through. Remove from heat assemble sandwiches by placing each cutlet on a roll evenly top each with lettuce and tomato then serve.

Thanksgiving Sandwiches – Makes 4 sandwiches

- **16 slices mesquite turkey breast (lunchmeat)**
- **1 cup whole fresh cranberries**
- **½ cup granulated sugar**
- **2 teaspoons orange juice**
- **6 Tablespoons jar chicken gravy**
- **4 slices provolone cheese**
- **8 slices French bread**

Tip

The recipe calls for basting bread with chicken gravy in step 2 & 3 so the gravy needs to separate by 3 Tablespoons. The first 3 Tablespoons is used to baste the bread in step 2 and the finally 3 Tablespoons used to baste the bread in step 3.

Instructions:

1. Rinse cranberries then in a medium non-stick pan sprayed with no-stick add cranberries cook over medium-low heat for about 2 minutes. Add sugar as well as orange juice to cranberries stirring everything together continues to cook for 3 minutes or until cranberries start to break up. Turn heat off then mash cranberries together with back of spatula set aside until needed.
2. Preheat an indoor grill on medium heat then start to assemble sandwiches by taking 2 slices of French breads and baste one piece with a small amount of chicken gravy and spread with small amount of cranberry sauce on another piece of bread repeat with remaining pieces of bread until you have 4 slices basted with gravy and 4 slices with cranberry sauce.
3. Place bread on heated grill gravy side down then top with 4 slices of turkey a slice of provolone then top with cranberry piece of bread with the cranberry sauce facing down on top the cheese. Repeat with reaming sandwiches and once sandwiches are assembled on the grill baste the top pieces

of the sandwiches with the remaining chicken gravy. Let sandwiches grill for 5 minutes on each side then remove and serve.

Western Cheeseburgers – Makes 4 serving

- **1 pound ground beef**
- **½ cup BBQ sauce**
- **8 strips peppered bacon**
- **4 slices of Colby cheese**
- **ground black pepper**
- **onion straws recipe (see page 171)**
- **4 onion rolls**

Instructions:

1. Take ground beef and form into 4 patties season each patty with ground black pepper.
2. Heat grill on medium-high heat and cook burgers on direct heat for 20-25 minutes or until your preferred doneness turning burgers once half way through. Melt cheese on burgers last 5 minutes of cooking.
3. Cook bacon in a medium skillet on medium-low heat for 10 minutes or until bacon is crisp.
4. Once burgers are cooked let them sit for a minute while warming up the BBQ sauce.
5. Assemble burgers by placing the cheeseburger on the bun followed by 2 strips of bacon, some onions straws, and evenly drizzle BBQ sauce over burger then serve.

Turkey Burgers – Makes 4 serving

- **1 pound ground turkey**
- **¼ cup fine diced sweet onion**
- **3 ½ Tablespoons steak sauce**
- **dashes hickory smoked salt**
- **4 slices white American cheese**
- **4 onion rolls**
- **lettuce leaves**

Instructions:

1. In a medium mixing bowl mix together ground turkey, onion, and steak sauce making sure onions and steak sauce are mixed together completely with turkey meat.
2. Form into 4 patties then place on plate and sprinkle some hickory smoked salt each side of the patties.
3. Heat grill on medium to high heat and cook burgers over direct heat for around 20 minutes turning only once halfway through. The last 5-8 minutes move to indirect heat and finish cooking until no pink in the middle. The last minutes add cheese and let melt then remove from heat. Place on onion roll top with lettuce and any other condiments then serve.

French Onion Turkey Burgers – Makes 4 servings

- 1 pound ground turkey
- 1 Tablespoon Worcestershire
- 1 Tablespoon red wine
- 1 Tablespoon diced sweet onion
- ¼ cup can French onion soup plus 3 Tablespoons
- ¼ cup plain panko bread crumbs
- dashes ground black pepper
- 1 medium tomato (sliced)
- 4 lettuce leaves
- 4 sliced white American cheese
- 4 English muffins

Instructions:

1. In a large mixing bowl mix together turkey, wine, Worcestershire, onion, bread crumbs, black pepper, and 3 Tablespoons French onion soup. Once thoroughly mixed form 4 patties about ¼ pound each then place in refrigerator for 2 hours.
2. Heat the grill on medium-high heat then grill burgers over direct heat for 20-25 minutes or until cooked through turning once halfway through. The last 10 minutes baste with ¼ cup French onion soup. The last 5 minutes melt cheese then remove from heat and serve with rolls, tomato, and lettuce.

Pork Burgers- Makes 4 burgers

- 1 pound ground pork
- ¼ cup diced yellow onion
- ½ teaspoon mesquite liquid smoke
- 1 Tablespoon BBQ rub (see page 191)
- 1 teaspoon yellow mustard
- ½ teaspoon Worcestershire sauce
- 3 Tablespoons plain bread crumbs
- 3 slices of yellow American cheese
- dashes ground black pepper
- 4 whole wheat hamburger rolls

Tip

      The burgers are going to be grilled over direct heat and they have cheese inside them which may cause flare-ups. In the case of flare-ups turn heat all the way down and move burgers to in-direct heat or a top rack of grill. If flare-ups become a problem then finish cooking burgers over in-direct heat or top rack and increase the cook time by another 10 minutes or until juices run clear.

Make Ahead

      Take the sliced of American cheese and cut into small cubes then set aside.

Instructions:

1. Preheat grill on medium-high heat. In a large mixing bowl combine the first six ingredients making sure to mix everything together. Once those are mixed together then mix in the bread crumbs, cubes of American cheese, and ground black pepper.
2. Form 4 patties about ¼ pound each then place on heat grill over direct heat and cook for 25-30 minutes or until juices run clear. Once cook remove from heat place on hamburger buns and serve with lettuce and tomato if desired.

Salads

Spinach Salad w/Hot Bacon Dressing – Makes 4 servings

- **4 cups bag baby spinach (stems remove)**
- **8 cherry tomatoes**
- **½ cup can whole black olives**
- **¾ cup bag seasoned croutons**

Bacon Dressing

- **½ cup olive oil**
- **½ teaspoon bottled minced garlic**
- **1 ½ Tablespoons fine diced yellow onion**
- **2 ½ strips turkey bacon**
- **¼ cup red wine vinegar**
- **1 ½ teaspoon Dijon mustard**
- **dashes sea salt**
- **dashes ground black pepper**
- **dashes Italian seasoning**

Tip

The bacon dressing recipe makes ¾ cup. Double recipe if one wants more dressing or can be cut in half for less dressing.

Instructions:

1. Cook turkey bacon in a small non stick pan for about 7 8 minutes or until bacon is cooked through turning once. Remove bacon from pan set aside. Once cooled crumble bacon set aside.
2. In a small pot over low heat add crumbled bacon, onion, and garlic cook for 3 minutes stirring occasionally. Add remaining bacon dressing ingredients to pot whisking everything together. Let dressing cook for 3-5 minutes on low heat or until warm stirring occasionally.
3. Remove dressing from heat and cover until ready to use. Rinse the cherry tomatoes then cut into quarters set aside. Rinse spinach then in a large mixing bowl add spinach, tomatoes, olives, croutons and bacon dressing tossing everything together then serve.

Shrimp Fajita Salad – Makes 4 servings

- **24 extra large raw shrimp (veins removed and shells removed including tail shells)**
- **1 ½ teaspoons mesquite liquid smoke**
- **1 Tablespoon Worcestershire**
- **1 Tablespoon fajita seasoning**
- **6 cups bag baby spinach (rinsed with stems removed)**
- **¼ cup can black beans**
- **¼ cup can corn**
- **¼ cup diced yellow onion**
- **10 cherry tomatoes (rinsed)**
- **½ cup can black olives**
- **1 ¼ Tablespoon lime juice**
- **1/3 – ½ cup Italian dressing**
- **bag tortilla strips**

Make Ahead

Rinse shrimp pat dry then in a small bowl whisk together liquid smoke, Worcestershire and fajita seasoning pour mixture into a bag and add shrimp. Make sure all shrimp get covered with fajita seasoning mixture let marinate in refrigerator for 4-6 hours.

Instructions:

1. Dice cherry tomatoes put into a small pot with the black beans, corn, onion and lime juice stirring everything together warm up mixture on low heat cover and turn heat off keep cover until needed.
2. In a large non-stick pan sprayed with no-stick cook shrimp over medium-low heat for 5-7 minutes or until shrimp are opaque remove from heat set aside.
3. In an extra large mixing bowl toss together the spinach, black olives and Italian dressing then evenly place spinach mixture into salad bowls about 1 ½ cup per salad. Evenly top each salad with black bean mixture about 2 ½ -3 tablespoons then top with shrimp around 6 for each salad. Finally, top each salad with some tortilla strips and serve.

Tuna Salad w/Lemon Vinaigrette – Makes 4 servings

- 2 (5ounce) can of tuna in water (drained)
- ¼ cup light mayonnaise
- 2 Tablespoons diced sweet onion
- 1/8 teaspoon garlic powder
- 1/8 teaspoon paprika
- 1/8 teaspoon salt
- 1/8 teaspoon ground black pepper
- 2 medium tomatoes (cut into wedges)
- ½ cup can sliced black olives
- 6 cups bag romaine lettuce (rinsed) (1 ½ cups per salad)
- ½ bag seasoned croutons

Vinaigrette
- ¼ cup olive oil
- 2 Tablespoons red wine vinegar
- ¼ cup bottled lemon juice
- ½ teaspoon bottled minced garlic
- 1 teaspoon Dijon mustard
- dashes sea salt
- dashes ground black pepper

Instructions:

1. In a medium mixing bowl whisk together the vinaigrette ingredients set aside then mix together the tuna with mayonnaise, diced onion, garlic powder, paprika, salt, and pepper.
2. In an extra large mixing bowl toss together romaine lettuce with vinaigrette then evenly spoon lettuce into four salad bowls and evenly top each with tuna mixture placed in the middle. Add to each tuna topped salad some tomatoes, black olives, and croutons then serve.

Chicken Fajita Salad – Makes 4 servings

- **2 boneless skinless chicken breast**
- **½ cup fajita seasoning**
- **6 Tablespoons Worcestershire**
- **2 Tablespoons mesquite liquid smoke**
- **6 cups bag baby spinach (rinsed with stems removed)**
- **¼ cup can black beans**
- **¼ cup can corn**
- **¼ cup diced yellow onion**
- **10 cherry tomatoes (rinsed)**
- **½ cup can black olives**
- **1 ¼ Tablespoon lime juice**
- **1/3 – ½ cup Italian dressing**
- **bag tortilla strips**

Make Ahead

In a glass measuring cup whisk together fajita seasoning, Worcestershire and liquid smoke together set aside. Rinse chicken breast then butterfly each breast place in a large plastic resealable bag pour fajita seasoning mixture over chicken making sure to cover all of each breast. Place in refrigerator to marinate overnight.

Instructions:

1. Dice cherry tomatoes put into a small pot with the black beans, corn, onion and lime juice stirring everything together warm up mixture on low heat cover and turn heat off keep cover until needed.
2. Heat grill add chicken to grill cook over direct heat for 20-30 minutes or until chicken is cooked through remove from heat and cut into strips.
3. In a large mixing bowl toss together baby spinach with Italian dressing and black olives then evenly spoon spinach mixture into four salad bowls about 1 ½ cup per salad. Evenly spoon on top of the spinach the black bean mixture then top each with some chicken. Finally, top salads with tortilla strips and serve.

Chicken Taco Salad – Makes 4 servings

- 1 large boneless chicken breast
- 5 Tablespoons plain panko bread crumbs
- 2 Tablespoons packaged taco seasoning
- 1 medium tomato
- ¼ cup can sliced black olives
- ¼ can black beans
- 1 egg
- 1 Tablespoon low-fat milk
- ½ cup bag tortilla strips
- 1/3 cup bag shredded Colby & jack cheese
- ¾ cup Italian dressing
- 1 teaspoon green hot sauce
- 6 cups bag mixed greens lettuce (1 ½ cup per salad)

Tip

There is going to be one chicken strip per salad so if more chicken is desired then double chicken breast as well as bread crumbs, taco seasoning, egg, and milk.

Instructions:

1. In a medium shallow dish mix together bread crumbs with taco seasoning set aside. Preheat oven on 350 degrees then cut chicken into four strips. In another shallow dish whisk together egg with milk.
2. Dip each chicken strip into egg mixture then dredge in bread crumb mixture making sure to coat each side of strips. Place bread strips on a medium baking pan sprayed with no-stick and place in oven for 25-30 minutes or until chicken is cooked through. Let sit for 5 minutes then cut each strip into pieces.
3. Dice tomato set aside until needed. In a large mixing bowl toss together lettuce, dressing, hot sauce, and diced tomatoes then evenly spoon into four salad bowls. Top each salad with a Tablespoon of black beans then evenly top with black olives. Finally, top salads with chicken one cut-up strip per salad and evenly top with cheese as well as evenly top with tortilla strips serve.

BBQ Chicken Ranch Salad – Makes 4 salads

- 1 boneless skinless chicken breast
- ¼ teaspoon paprika
- ¼ teaspoon hickory smoked salt
- ¼ teaspoon garlic powder
- ¼ teaspoon onion powder
- 1 teaspoon light brown sugar
- 2 Tablespoons bottled BBQ sauce
- ½ cup can medium whole black olives (drained)
- ¼ cup can corn (drained)
- 1 medium tomato
- 5 ½ -6 Tablespoons bottled ranch dressing
- 6 cups bag romaine lettuce (rinsed)
- 1 French rolls
- 2 Tablespoons olive oil
- 1 Tablespoon ranch seasoning

Make Ahead

Mix together paprika, smoked salt, garlic powder, onion powder, and brown sugar together set aside. Rinse chicken then cut into 4 strips and rub paprika mixture all over chicken strips place in refrigerator to marinate for 4 hours.

Instructions:

1. Rinse tomato then dice up place in refrigerator until needed. Preheat oven on 300 degrees then cut the French roll in half lengthwise and cut into strips then cut into cubes. Toss the cubes with olive oil and ranch seasoning. Place seasoned cubes on a small non-stick baking pan and let bake for 5-7 minutes or until cubes start to firm up but are still a little soft. Remove from oven set aside.
2. Preheat oven on 325 degrees then place chicken strips on a small non-stick baking pan and bake for 25-30 minutes or until chicken is no longer pink in the middle. The last 10 minutes of baking baste chicken with BBQ sauce. Remove

from oven let sit for a few minutes then cut each strip into cubes.

3. In a large mixing bowl toss together lettuce with ranch dressing and diced tomato. Spoon salad into four salad bowls about 1 ½ cup per salad. Top each salad with a Tablespoon of corn evenly top with black olives then top with chicken cubes about 1 strip per salad finish off with some ranch croutons and serve.

Taco Salad- Makes 4-6 servings

- **1 pound ground turkey**
- **1 package taco seasoning**
- **½ teaspoon chili powder**
- **2 teaspoons lime juice**
- **¼ cup diced yellow onion**
- **¼ cup can corn (drained)**
- **¼ cup diced tomato**
- **1 (2.25ounce) can sliced black olives**
- **1 1/3 cup crushed bag tortilla chips**
- **¾ cup French dressing**
- **1 cup shredded bag Colby & jack cheese**
- **1 avocado (cubed)**
- **dashes hot sauce**
- **¾ cup water**
- **6 cup romaine lettuce (rinsed)**

Instructions:

1. In a large non-stick pan brown turkey meat over medium heat then drain any excess fat. Once turkey is brown add taco seasoning, water, chili powder, lime juice, onion, tomato and corn stirring together. Bring to boil then turn heat down let simmer for 5 minutes stirring occasionally then remove from heat let sit for 5 minutes.
2. In a large mixing bowl add taco meat, olives, tortilla chips, dressing, cheese and hot sauce tossing everything together. Put about a ½ cup or so of lettuce in salads bowls then evenly top each with taco salad mixture then evenly top each with some cubed avocado and serve.

Roasted Zucchini Salad – Makes 5-8 servings

- **2 medium zucchinis**
- **14 cherry tomatoes**
- **¼ cup olive oil**
- **6 Tablespoons can corn (drained)**
- **1 1/3 cups can whole black olives (drained)**

Dressing

- **1/3 cup olive oil**
- **5 ½ Tablespoons balsamic vinegar**
- **1 teaspoon Dijon mustard**
- **½ teaspoon bottled minced garlic**
- **½ teaspoon diced shallots**
- **dashes sea salt**
- **dashes ground black pepper**

Croutons

- **3 slices French bread (cubed)**
- **2 ½ Tablespoons olive oil**
- **¼ teaspoon garlic powder**
- **¼ teaspoon onion powder**
- **¼ teaspoon paprika**
- **¼ teaspoon hickory smoked salt**
- **½ teaspoon light brown sugar**
- **¼ teaspoon ground black pepper**

Tip

I like to serve this salad on sliced tomato or sliced cucumber

Make Ahead

Mix together garlic powder, onion powder, paprika, smoked salt, black pepper and brown sugar it makes a good amount so keep leftover mixture in a container for next time. In a medium bowl toss together cubed French bread, olive oil, and garlic powder mixture. Place in oven on 300 degrees let bake for 5-8 minutes or until bread starts to firm up. Remove from oven set aside until needed.

Instructions:

1. Rinse zucchinis and rinse cherry tomatoes. Preheat oven on 325 degrees quarter the cherry tomatoes place in refrigerator until needed then cut off both ends of zucchinis and discard. Cut the zucchinis into cubes and toss with olive oil season with salt and pepper. Bake in oven for 35 minutes the last 10 minutes of baking add quartered tomatoes and corn. Remove from oven let sit while making the dressing.
2. Whisk together dressing ingredients then in a large mixing bowl toss together zucchini, tomatoes, corn, olives, and croutons. Slowly toss in dressing might want to save some dressing for the side and serve.

Potato Salad – Makes 6-8 servings

- **5 red potatoes (rinsed and quartered)**
- **¼ cup diced yellow onion**
- **¼ cup cooked crumbled peppered bacon**
- **3 large hard boiled eggs**
- **3 ounces mayo**
- **3 ounces Dijon mustard**
- **1 teaspoon paprika**
- **1 teaspoon ground black pepper**

Instructions:

1. In a large pot boil quartered potatoes over medium heat for about 15 minutes or until potatoes are fork tender. Once potatoes are done strain and run under cool water for a few seconds
2. Let potatoes cool once potatoes are cool chop up each quartered potato and place in a large mixing bowl.
3. Using an egg slicer to slice the eggs and slice the eggs twice once in one direction then in the opposite direction then add egg to potatoes. Add the rest of the ingredients to the mixing bowl with the egg and potatoes then toss everything together making sure it is mixed thoroughly. Chill for a few hours before serving.

Antipasto Salad – Makes 6-8 servings

- 7 slices pepperoni
- 7 slices hard salami
- 4 slices honey ham
- ¼ cup sliced black olives
- ½ cup quartered cherry tomatoes
- 4 slices provolone cheese
- 4 slices Colby cheese
- 3 ounces diced onion
- 3 ounces diced red bell pepper
- 1 Vinaigrette recipe (see page 187)

Instructions:

1. Cut pepperoni, hard salami, honey ham, provolone, and Colby cheeses into thin strips.
2. In a large mixing bowl toss the strips of pepperoni, hard salami, honey ham, provolone, Colby cheeses, sliced olives, tomatoes, diced onion, diced red bell pepper, and vinaigrette together.
3. Place in a container and chill for 24 hours before serving. It can be served by itself or over some lettuce.

Pasta Salad – Makes 4-6 servings

- 1 ¼ cup penne pasta
- ¾ cup Italian dressing
- ¼ cup can diced garlic & olive oil tomatoes
- 2 cup water
- 1 Tablespoon can chopped black olives
- ½ cup fresh broccoli florets
- ¼ cup fresh grated parmesan cheese
- dashes ground black pepper
- dashes salt

Instructions:

1. In a medium pot bring 2 cups of water to boil then add salt and pasta lower heat to a low boil for about 10-15 minutes or until pasta is fork tender.
2. Drain pasta and run cold water over pasta for a few minutes or until pasta has cooled.
3. In a medium mixing bowl add pasta, tomatoes, dressing, olives, broccoli, parmesan, and black pepper and toss everything together.
4. Chill for a few hours before serving make sure to toss once more before serving.

Section 4

Main Dishes

Beef Dishes

Beef & Broccoli – Makes 3-4 servings

- **1 pound top sirloin**
- **2 ½ cups cut-up fresh broccoli**
- **2 teaspoons bottled minced garlic**
- **2 Tablespoons oil**
- **1 brown sauce recipe (see page 179)**

Instructions:

1. Cut sirloin into thin strips set aside and heat oil over medium-low heat in a large pan.
2. Once oil is heated add strips of sirloin and cook for 6-8 minutes until steak is no-longer pink.
3. Remove steak from pan and set aside then add broccoli and minced garlic sauté for 1-2 minutes continually stirring so garlic does not burn.
4. Add steak back to pan with broccoli then add brown sauce stirring everything together and sauté for another 1-2 minutes stirring continually then remove from heat and serve over rice.

Lemon Steak Stir-Fry – Makes 4-5 servings

- **1 pound steak (pre-cut packaged stir-fry strips usually two packages)**
- **½ cup yellow onion strips**
- **1 ½ cup broccoli florets**
- **½ cup green bell pepper strips**
- **2 teaspoons bottled minced garlic**
- **½ cup all-purpose flour**
- **2 Tablespoons olive oil**
- **dashes sea salt**
- **dashes ground black pepper**
- **lemon sauce recipe (see page 180)**

Make Ahead
The lemon sauce will need to be doubled for this recipe and should be made ahead of time. Once sauce is done keep warm by covering and turn heat off so it does not over cook sauce.

Instructions:

1. Mix together flour with salt and pepper set aside. Heat olive oil in an extra large pan over medium heat then dredge the strips of beef in the flour add to the pan and cook for 5 minutes turning once halfway through cooking.
2. Remove steak from pan set aside. Add the garlic, broccoli, bell pepper and onion to pan stirring frequently let cook for 2-3 minutes then add steak as well as sauce to pan stirring everything together. Let mixture cook for a minute then remove from heat and serve.

Steak w/Mushrooms – Makes 4 servings

- **4 thin cut New York steaks**
- **2 cups sliced fresh button mushrooms**
- **2 teaspoons bottled minced garlic**
- **1 Tablespoon lemon juice**
- **2 Tablespoons red wine**
- **1 Tablespoon margarine**
- **¼ cup crumbled bleu cheese**
- **dashes salt**
- **dashes ground black pepper**

Instructions:

1. In a large pan melt margarine over medium heat then add mushrooms and season with salt and pepper. Cook mushrooms for 6-8 minutes stirring occasionally.
2. Add minced garlic, lemon juice, and red wine to mushrooms stirring everything together continue to cook for another 3-5 minutes or until mushrooms start to caramelize. Stir in bleu cheese then turn off heat and cover.
3. Heat grill to medium-high heat and season steaks with ground black pepper then grill for 6-8 minutes turning once halfway through steaks will be rare to medium rare cook longer for well done steaks. Remove steaks from grill place on platter and evenly spoon mushroom mixture over steaks then serve.

Steak Chili – Makes 4-6 servings

- **1 ½ pound top sirloin**
- **1 fully-cooked andouille sausage**
- **½ cup diced red bell pepper**
- **½ cup diced yellow onion**
- **2 teaspoons bottled minced garlic**
- **2 cans plain stewed tomatoes**
- **1 teaspoon mesquite liquid smoke**
- **2 teaspoons chili powder**
- **1 teaspoon tomato paste**
- **2 teaspoons Worcestershire**
- **1 teaspoon yellow mustard**
- **dashes salt**
- **dashes ground black pepper**
- **dashes green hot sauce**

Tip

This is a spicy dish.

Instructions:

1. Drain the cans of stewed tomatoes reserving the juice in a container then chop up the stewed tomatoes adding them to container with the reserved juice place in refrigerator until ready to use.
2. Dice up the steak and andouille sausage then place in a medium pot over medium-low heat and cook for 6 minutes stirring continually. Cover pot with lid and continue to cook for another 3-4 minutes stirring occasionally.
3. Remove the steak and sausage from pot set aside in a bowl. Add the onion, bell pepper, garlic, and chili powder to the pot stirring everything together continue to cook for 2-3 minutes with out the lid.
4. Add the steak mixture, liquid smoke, Worcestershire, yellow mustard, stewed tomatoes with the juice, tomato paste, salt, pepper, and hot sauce to pot with the onion

mixture stirring everything together.

5. Bring mixture to boil let boil for a minute then turn the heat down to low cover the pot with the lid and let simmer for one hour stirring occasionally.

6. After the hour, remove the chili from the heat let sit for a minute or so then serve with sour cream or tortilla chips.

Pepper Steak – Makes 3-4 servings

- **1 ¾ pound top sirloin**
- **1 cup yellow onion strips**
- **½ cup red bell pepper strips**
- **½ cup greed bell pepper strips**
- **2 teaspoons bottled minced garlic**
- **1 Tablespoon soy sauce**
- **2 Tablespoons red wine**
- **2 teaspoons Worcestershire sauce**
- **½ teaspoon mesquite liquid smoke**
- **2 Tablespoons olive oil**
- **salt**
- **ground black pepper**

Instructions:

1. Cut the sirloin in half then cut into thin strips and season lightly with ground black pepper on both sides. Heat olive oil in a large non-stick pan over medium-low heat then add steak and cook for 2-3 minutes turning in order to cook both sides.
2. Add the onion, bell peppers, and garlic to pan with steak stirring everything together continue to cook for 1 minute. Add liquid smoke, Worcestershire, soy, and red wine to pan season with salt and ground pepper stirring everything together and continue to cook for 2-3 minutes and remove from heat then serve.

Steak Fajitas – Makes 4-6 servings

- **2 pounds top sirloin**
- **2/3 cup green bell pepper thin strips**
- **2/3 cup yellow onion thin strips**
- **½ teaspoon fajita seasoning**
- **2/3 cup bag baby spinach**
- **1 teaspoon bottled minced garlic**
- **2 teaspoons bottled lime juice**
- **2 Tablespoons olive oil**
- **4-6 soft taco size flour tortillas**

Make Ahead
Season top sirloin evenly with fajita seasoning on both sides then put in refrigerator to marinate for 6 hours.

Instructions:

1. Remove stems and rinse baby spinach put in refrigerator until needed. Cut steak in half then thinly slice. Heat olive oil in a large non-stick pan over medium-low heat then add sliced steak. Cook for 5 minutes making sure to brown on both sides.
2. Remove steak from pan and set aside. Drain any excess fat from pan then add onion, bell pepper, and garlic to pan; cook for 2-3 minutes then add steak and lime juice to pan stirring everything together continue to cook for 2-3 minutes. Remove from heat.
3. Assemble fajitas by evenly spooning meat mixture in tortillas then evenly top with spinach wrap and serve.

Beef & Pasta – Makes 4-5 servings

- 1 ¼ pound top sirloin
- 1 ¾ cup uncooked bow tie pasta
- 1 ½ cup fresh broccoli florets
- 1 (6.5ounce) can sliced mushrooms
- 1/3 cup yellow onion strips
- 1/3 cup all-purpose flour
- 1 teaspoon bottled minced garlic
- 2 cups low-sodium beef broth
- 2 Tablespoons olive oil
- 2 Tablespoons red wine
- 1 Tablespoon margarine
- dashes sea salt
- dashes ground black pepper
- brown sauce recipe (see page 179)

Tip

The brown sauce recipe needs to be doubled for this dish. Make the brown sauce ahead and add 2 Tablespoons of red wine is to be whisked into the brown sauce. Once the sauce is made leave cover and leave on stove until ready to use.

Instructions:

1. Cut beef into small cubes place in refrigerator until ready to use. Bring beef broth to boil then add the pasta turn heat down some; let cook for 12-15 minutes or until pasta is tender stirring occasionally. Once pasta is done drain and stir in margarine cover until ready to use.
2. In a large non-stick pan heat olive oil over medium heat. Mix flour with some salt and pepper then dredge beef in flour coating both sides. Add beef to pan let cook for 6-8 minutes turning once halfway through that way both sides are brown.
3. Remove beef from pan then add broccoli, mushrooms, onion, and garlic to pan let cook for 5-6 minutes stirring

occasionally. Add beef, pasta, and sauce to pan stirring everything together then bring to boil. Once boiling low heat let cook for 2-3 minutes. Remove from heat and serve.

Beef & Noodles – Makes 5-7 servings

- 1 ¼ pound ground beef
- 2 cups uncooked egg noodles
- 2 cups low sodium beef broth
- 3 ½ Tablespoon red wine
- 1 Tablespoon Worcestershire
- 2 (4.5ounce) cans of sliced mushrooms
- ground black pepper
- brown sauce recipe (see page 179)

Tip

Once the dish is made by placing it in the refrigerator overnight will help the sauce blend with beef and noodles and enhance the flavor.

Make Ahead

The brown sauce recipe needs to be doubled for this dish. Make the brown sauce ahead and add 3 ½ Tablespoons of red wine is to be whisked into the brown sauce. Once the sauce is made leave cover and leave on stove until ready to use. The sauce recipe can be tripled if one would like the dish to have more sauce.

Instructions:

1. In a large pan cook ground beef over medium heat for 20-25 minutes or until ground beef is brown turn off the heat drain any fat then stir in Worcestershire with ground beef cover and set aside until needed.
2. Bring beef broth to boil then add the egg noodles let cook for 10-15 minutes or until noodles are fork tender. Once noodles are done drain then in a extra large mixing bowl add the ground beef, noodles, mushrooms and sauce stirring everything together season with black pepper and serve.

Beef Stew – Makes 4-6 servings

Marinade:
- ¾ pound thinly sliced eye of round steak
- 2 ½ Tablespoon fajita seasoning
- 3 teaspoons mesquite liquid smoke
- 6 Tablespoons Worcestershire

Stew Ingredients:
- 1 medium white potatoes (rinsed)
- 1 medium carrots (peeled & rinsed)
- 1 small zucchini (rinsed–cut off both ends and discard)
- 1/3 cup chopped sweet onion
- 1 teaspoon bottled minced garlic
- ¼ cup can Italian diced tomatoes
- 2 ½ cups low-sodium beef broth
- 2 Tablespoon red wine
- 1 teaspoon steak sauce
- 1 teaspoon Worcestershire
- 2 Tablespoons olive oil
- ¾ cup all-purpose flour
- dashes sea salt
- dashes ground black pepper
- dashes Italian seasoning

Make Ahead

In a small mixing bowl whisk together fajita seasoning, liquid smoke, and Worcestershire then place steak into a resealable plastic bag pour marinade over steak place in refrigerator for 4-5 hours. Cut carrots and zucchini into cubes place in refrigerator until needed.

Instructions:

1. In a gallon size resealable bag mix together flour with salt and pepper then remove steak from marinade pat dry and cut into cubes. In a large pot heat olive oil over medium then add cubed steak to bag with flour shake to coat.

2. Add coated steak to large pot to brown let cook for 2 minutes then add onion and garlic to pan continue to cook for 3 minutes then cut potato into cubes add to pan along with the rest of the stew ingredients stir everything together bring to boil then turn heat down to low cover and let simmer for 3-4 hours.

3. The last ½ hour stir together 3 tablespoons of flour with some water and stir into stew to help it thicken up. Once the 3-4 hours are done give the stew a good stir then remove from heat and serve.

Poultry Dishes

Chicken Enchiladas – Makes 4-5 enchiladas

- **1 pound boneless chicken breast (rinse chicken)**
- **1 ½ - 2 Tablespoons fajita seasoning**
- **¼ cup diced yellow onion**
- **¼ cup diced red bell pepper**
- **¼ cup diced tomato**
- **1 Tablespoon bottled lime juice**
- **½ cup red mild enchilada sauce**
- **½ cup shredded Colby & jack cheese**
- **4-5 flour tortillas soft taco size**

Make Ahead

Cut chicken breasts in halve then cut into thin strips then evenly sprinkle each side with fajita seasoning then place in a resealable bag in refrigerator for 4 hours.

Instructions:

1. In a medium non-stick pan sauté onion and bell pepper over medium-low for 2-3 minutes then add tomato and lime juice continue to cook for another minute. Remove onion mixture from pan and set aside in a bowl then replace pan to heat and add chicken.
2. Cook chicken over medium-low heat for 10-15 minutes or until chicken is no longer pink in the middle turning throughout cooking so chicken does not burn.
3. Preheat oven on 325 degrees then assemble enchiladas by placing about 4-5 strips of chicken in each tortilla towards one end then evenly top with onion mixture.
4. Roll chicken filled tortillas and in a medium baking pan sprayed with no-stick pour ¼ cup of enchilada sauce in the bottom then add the rolled chicken filled tortilla in baking pan.
5. Top the tortillas with the remaining enchilada sauce then evenly sprinkle cheese on top of the tortillas then place in oven for around 5-7 minutes or until cheese is melts. Remove from oven let stand for a few minutes then serve.

Chicken w/Mushrooms – Makes 4 serving

- **4 boneless skinless chicken breast (rinse chicken)**
- **1/3 cup all-purpose flour**
- **½ teaspoon salt**
- **½ teaspoon ground black pepper**
- **1 ¼ Tablespoons dry white wine (cooking wine)**
- **1 (4ounce) can sliced mushrooms**
- **1 ¼ teaspoon bottled lemon juice**
- **1 teaspoon bottled minced garlic**
- **1 Tablespoon margarine**
- **¼ cup olive oil**
- **dashes salt**
- **dashes ground black pepper**

Instructions:

1. Mix together flour, ½ teaspoon salt, and ½ teaspoon ground black pepper on a large shallow bowl and set aside.
2. Butterfly each chicken breast then place between a large piece of plastic wrap and pound out using a meat mallet or rolling pin until chicken is around inch to inch and half thin. Repeat with remaining chicken.
3. In a large pan heat olive oil over medium-low heat then flour each piece of chicken both sides and add to oil. Cook for 15-20 minutes or until no pink in the middle turn chicken only once halfway through.
4. Once chicken is done remove from heat let drain on paper towel and pour out any excess oil from pan then return pan to heat on medium-low heat
5. Melt margarine then add mushrooms, garlic, dashes of salt and ground black pepper sauté for 3-5 minutes stirring occasionally. Add white wine and lemon juice and continue to cook for 2-3 minutes stirring occasionally. Place cooked chicken on a platter then evenly top with mushrooms and serve.

Balsamic & Honey Drumsticks – Makes 4 servings

- **8 fresh chicken drumsticks (rinse chicken)**
- **½ cup balsamic vinegar**
- **¾ cup honey**
- **2 ½ Tablespoons olive oil**

Make Ahead

      In large bowl whisk together vinegar, honey, and olive oil then pierce chicken with a fork. Place chicken in a plastic resealable bag and pour vinegar mixture over chicken let marinate in refrigerator for 8 hours.

Tip

      The drumsticks can also be grilled. Marinate the chicken the same as stated above. Right before grilling whisk together ¼ cup balsamic vinegar, 1/3-1/2 cup honey, 1 tablespoon of olive oil. The vinegar mixture will be used to baste the drumsticks while they are being grilled. Grill them for 45-55 minutes or until juices run clear and no longer pink in the middle.

Instructions:

1. Preheat oven on 350 degrees. Discard marinated and place drumsticks on a large baking pan sprayed with no-stick. Place in oven and bake for 45-55 minutes or until juices run clear and no longer pink in the middle. Remove drumsticks from oven let sit for a few minutes then serve.

Chicken Parmesan – Makes 4 chicken parmesan

- **4 boneless skinless chicken breast (rinse chicken)**
- **2/3 cup plain bread crumbs**
- **½ teaspoon paprika**
- **2 teaspoons bottled grated parmesan cheese**
- **1/3 cup milk**
- **1 egg**
- **1 cup seasoned tomato sauce**
- **½ cup bag shredded cheddar cheese**
- **dashes ground black pepper**

Instructions:

1. In a shallow dish mix together bread crumbs with paprika, parmesan cheese, and black pepper then set aside. Preheat oven on 350 degrees then whisk together milk and egg and pour into another shallow dish.
2. Dip each piece of chicken into egg wash coating both sides then dredge in bread crumb mixture making sure to cover each piece completely. Place on a large baking pan sprayed with no-stick and bake in oven for 25-30 minutes.
3. Remove chicken from oven then evenly top each piece with tomato sauce and cheese then place back in oven to cook for another 10 minutes then remove and serve.

Lemon Chicken Stir-Fry – Makes 4-6 servings

- **4 boneless skinless chicken breast (rinse chicken)**
- **½ cup thinly sliced red bell pepper strips**
- **½ cup thinly sliced yellow onion strips**
- **½ cup can baby corn**
- **2 teaspoons bottled minced garlic**
- **2-3 tablespoons olive oil**
- **1/3 cup all-purpose flour**
- **dashes salt**
- **dashes ground black pepper**
- **lemon sauce recipe (see page 180)**

Instructions:

1. Following directions make lemon sauce. Keep covered over low heat until needed.
2. Cut chicken breast into medium size cubes. In a shallow bowl mix flour with some dashes of salt and pepper.
3. Heat olive oil over medium-low heat in a large pan. Dredge the cubes of chicken in the flour mixture and add coated chicken to pan.
4. Cook chicken for 10-15 minutes or until chicken is no longer pink in the middle turning once halfway through. Once chicken is cook remove from pan and set aside in a bowl.
5. Add the onion, bell pepper, corn, and garlic to pan sauté for 2-4 minutes then add chicken back to pan stirring everything together.
6. Add the lemon sauce to the pan stirring everything together and let boil for 1-2 minutes stirring frequently. Remove from heat and serve over rice.

Orange Chicken Stir-Fry – Makes 4-6 servings

- **4 boneless skinless chicken breast (rinse chicken)**
- **½ cup baby carrots cut into matchsticks**
- **½ cup thin strips sliced yellow onion**
- **½ cup can baby corn**
- **2 teaspoons bottled minced garlic**
- **2-3 tablespoons olive oil**
- **1/3 cup all-purpose flour**
- **dashes salt**
- **dashes ground black pepper**
- **orange sauce recipe (see page 181)**

Instructions:

1. Following directions make orange sauce. Keep covered over low heat until needed.
2. Cut chicken breast into medium size cubes. In a shallow bowl mix flour with some dashes of salt and pepper.
3. Heat olive oil over medium-low heat in a large skillet. Dredge the cubes of chicken in the flour mixture and add coated chicken to pan.
4. Cook chicken for 10-15 minutes or until chicken is no longer pink in the middle turning once halfway through. Once chicken is cook remove from pan and put in a bowl then set aside.
5. Add the onion, carrots, corn, and garlic to pan sauté for 2-4 minutes then add chicken back to pan stirring everything together.
6. Add orange sauce to pan stirring everything together then bring mixture to boil and let boil for 1-2 minute stirring frequently. Remove from heat and serve with rice.

Chicken & Broccoli Stir-Fry- Makes 4-6 servings

- **2 boneless skinless chicken breast (rinse chicken)**
- **3 cups fresh broccoli florets**
- **½ cup thinly sliced strips yellow onion**
- **2 teaspoons bottled minced garlic**
- **1 ½ Tablespoon margarine**
- **1 ½ Tablespoons all-purpose flour**
- **1 ½ cups chicken broth**
- **2 teaspoon soy sauce**
- **2 Tablespoons olive oil**
- **dashes salt**
- **dashes ground black pepper**

Instructions:

1. In a small pot melt margarine over low heat then whisk in flour until absorbed by margarine. Add the chicken broth and soy sauce to pot whisking everything together until flour is absorbed by the broth. Bring broth to a boil whisking continually once broth is boiling turn heat off and cover.
2. Cut chicken breast into cubes about ½ inch to inch thick set aside. Heat olive oil in a large non-stick pan over medium heat then add chicken to pan and season with ground black pepper and salt. Cook chicken for 10-15 minutes or until cooked through and browned on both sides.
3. Remove chicken from pan by placing in a bowl and set aside. Add broccoli, onion, and garlic to pan stirring everything continue to cook for 5-6 minutes stirring frequently.
4. Add chicken back to pan stirring everything together then add the chicken sauce to pan stirring everything together. Bring chicken mixture to boil stirring frequently and once sauce starts to thicken then remove from heat and serve over rice or by itself.

Chicken & Black Bean Ravioli – Makes 16 raviolis

- 1 boneless skinless chicken breast (rinse chicken)
- ½ teaspoon fajita seasoning
- ¼ cup can black beans
- ½ cup bag baby spinach
- ¼ cup diced yellow onion
- ¼ cup diced red bell pepper
- 1 teaspoon margarine
- 1 Tablespoon bottled grated parmesan cheese
- 1 cup water
- 1 teaspoon chicken granules bouillon
- dashes salt
- dashes ground black pepper
- 32 wonton skins
- 1 light chunky tomato sauce recipe (see page 185)

Make Ahead
Sprinkle ½ teaspoon fajita seasoning evenly on both sides of the chicken breast then place in a plastic sandwich bag and put into refrigerator for 4 hours.

Instructions:

1. Preheat oven on 325 degrees. Placed seasoned chicken on a small non-stick baking pan then bake for 30-35 minutes or until chicken is cooked through. Remove chicken from heat let sit for 5 minutes then dice up the chicken breast.
2. Remove stems from baby spinach then rinse spinach and chop up spinach. In a small pot bring water to boil then stir in chicken granules. Once dissolved turn off heat and cover.
3. In a medium pan melt margarine over medium-low heat then add onions, bell pepper, and black beans season with salt & pepper. Cook for 5 minutes stirring frequently then add cooked diced chicken, spinach, and grated parmesan

to pan stirring everything together continue to cook for 1-2 minutes. Remove mixture from heat.

4. Start to assemble the ravioli by taking one wonton skin place about 2-3 teaspoons of mixture into the middle of the wonton then wet all four edges with a little of water then take another wonton skin place on top pressing down to seal all the edges. Using the back edges of a fork press down to help seal edges better. Repeat until all mixture and wonton skins are used. Place finished wontons under a damp cloth to keep them from drying out while assembling the raviolis.

5. In a large pan over medium-low heat place about ¼ cups to 1/3 cup of broth into pan. Once broth is warmed up then add about 4 raviolis at a time cover and let cook for 5-6 minutes then remove from pan place on a plate continue this process until all raviolis are cooked and add broth as needed during cooking process.

6. Once all raviolis are cooked place on a platter top with light chunky tomato sauce and serve.

Baked Chicken w/Mushroom gravy – Makes 4 chicken breasts

- **4 boneless skinless chicken breast (rinse chicken)**
- **1 cup plain bread crumbs**
- **½ teaspoon ground black pepper**
- **1 teaspoon garlic powder**
- **1 teaspoon onion powder**
- **1/3 cup milk**
- **1 beaten egg**
- **½ mushroom recipe (see page 161)**
- **brown sauce recipe (see page 179)**

Instructions:

1. In a large shallow dish mix together the bread crumbs, garlic powder, onion powder, and ground black pepper then set aside. Preheat oven on 350 degrees. Butterfly each chicken breast then place each chicken breast between plastic wrap and pound out chicken starting from the center working outwards; repeat process with remaining chicken breast then set aside.
2. In another large shallow dish whisk together the milk with the beaten egg. Take the pounded out chicken breast and dip into milk mixture coating both side then dredge through the bread crumb mixture coating both sides; repeat with remaining chicken breast then place on large non-stick baking pan.
3. Place chicken in oven letting bake for 35-40 minutes or until juice run clear. Turn chicken once halfway through baking time that way both side get a nice brown crust.
4. While chicken is baking, make the mushrooms and once mushrooms are finish dice up the mushrooms and set aside. The next step is to make the brown sauce and once the brown sauce is made add the diced mushrooms and let simmer for 5 minutes.
5. Once chicken is done then place chicken on plates and evenly top with mushroom sauce then serve.

Chicken & Noodles – Makes 4-6 servings

- 2 boneless skinless chicken breast (rinse chicken)
- 3 ½ cups uncooked egg noodles
- 2 (4ounce) cans sliced mushrooms
- 2 (8ounce) cans sliced carrots
- 4 cups low sodium chicken broth
- ½ cup all-purpose flour
- 2 Tablespoons olive oil
- 2 Tablespoons margarine
- 2 teaspoons minced garlic
- dashes sea salt
- dashes ground black pepper
- lemon sauce recipe (see page 180)

Tip

Make lemon sauce ahead and keep covered on low heat until needed.

Instructions:

1. Cut chicken breast into cubes then place in refrigerator until needed. In a large pot bring chicken broth to boil then add egg noodles turn heat down to medium-low let noodles boil for 12-15 minutes or until tender stirring occasionally. Drain noodles add margarine stirring together so noodles do not stick and set aside until needed.
2. In a shallow bowl mix together flour with salt and pepper. In a large non-stick pan heat olive oil over medium heat. Dredge chicken through flour then add to pan cook for 12-15 minutes or until chicken is longer pink inside. Be sure to turn chicken only once that way both sides get brown.
3. Once chicken is cook remove from pan set aside then add mushrooms, carrots, and garlic to pan let cook for 5-7 minutes. Add chicken, cooked noodles, and lemon sauce to pan stirring everything together. Bring mixture to boil then low heat and let simmer for 2-3 minutes stirring occasionally. Remove from heat and serve.

Chicken & Bean Chili – Makes 4-6 servings

- 1 large boneless skinless chicken breast (rinse chicken)
- 3 Tablespoons diced yellow onion
- 3 Tablespoons diced green bell pepper
- 1 (4.5ounce) can regular stewed tomatoes
- 2 teaspoons chili powder
- 2 teaspoons Worcestershire sauce
- 1 (15.5ounce) can red beans
- 1 cup bag baby spinach
- 1 teaspoon liquid smoke
- ½ teaspoon bottled minced garlic
- ¼ teaspoon fajita seasoning
- 1 ½ teaspoon tomato paste
- 1 ½ teaspoon yellow mustard
- 1 ½ teaspoon Dijon mustard
- dashes sea salt
- dashes ground black pepper
- dashes green hot sauce

Instructions:

1. Cut chicken into cubes then season with fajita seasoning then place in refrigerator until ready to use. Open stewed tomatoes reserving the juice then chop up the stewed tomatoes and place tomatoes along with reserved tomato juice in refrigerator until ready to use. Rinse baby spinach and remove stems place in refrigerator until ready to use.
2. Heat a large pot sprayed with no-stick over medium heat add chicken to pot and cover let cook for 6-7 minutes or until no longer pink stirring occasionally. Remove chicken from pot then add onion, garlic, bell pepper, and chili powder stirring everything together and let cook for 2-3 minutes.
3. Add tomatoes, reserved tomato juice, Worcestershire, drained beans, liquid smoke, tomato paste, yellow mustard, hot sauce, and Dijon mustard to pot season with salt and

pepper stirring everything together. Shred the cooked chicken then add the shredded chicken to the pot; bring chili mixture to boil then turn heat down to low cover and let simmer for one hour stirring occasionally.

4. The last 10 minutes stir in the baby spinach and season with salt and pepper as needed continue to cook for another 10 minutes then remove from heat and serve.

Dijon-Honey Chicken Tenders – Makes 4-6 servings

- **4 boneless skinless chicken breast**
- **3 ½ ounces Dijon mustard**
- **1 ½ Tablespoons honey**
- **1 egg**
- **¼ cup low-fat milk**
- **½ plain bread crumbs**

Make Ahead

Rinse chicken breast then cut into strip there should be about 4 strips per chicken breast place in refrigerator until ready to use.

Instructions:

1. Place bread crumbs in a shallow bowl then in another shallow bowl whisk together milk and egg set aside. Preheat oven on 350 degrees.
2. Whisk together the Dijon mustard and honey together in a medium mixing bowl and set aside. Take each chicken strip and dip into the milk mixture then dredge through the bread crumbs and place each bread chicken strip on a large baking pan sprayed with no-stick and once all chicken strips are bread place in oven bake for 30-35 minutes.
3. After the first 15 minutes, evenly baste each chicken strip with the Dijon mixture on both sides then place back in oven. Turn heat up to 375 degrees and finish baking chicken for another 15-20 minutes or until cooked through. Remove from heat and serve.

Parmesan and Pepper Chicken Tenders – Makes 2 servings

- 2 boneless skinless chicken breast
- 3 Tablespoons bottled grated parmesan cheese
- 1 teaspoon ground black pepper
- ½ cup plain bread crumbs
- 2 egg
- 1 ¼ Tablespoon cider vinegar
- dashes paprika

Tip

The tenders will be a little spicy double recipe for even more tasty tenders.

Make Ahead

Rinse chicken breast then cut into strip there should be about 4 strips per chicken breast place in refrigerator until ready to use.

Instructions:

1. In a medium shallow dish mix together the bread crumbs, parmesan cheese, pepper, and paprika then set aside. Preheat oven on 375 degrees then in another medium shallow dish whisk together egg with vinegar.
2. Dip each chicken strip in the egg mixture then dredge through the bread crumbs making sure to coat all sides. Place coated chicken strips on a large non-stick baking pan place in oven. Cook for 25-35 minutes or until cooked through turning once halfway through this way both sides get brown. Remove from oven and serve.

Chicken Thighs w/ Cranberry Sauce – Makes 4 servings

- **4 chicken thighs**
- **¾ cup Italian dressing**
- **1 ½ cups fresh whole cranberries**
- **2 Tablespoons balsamic vinegar**
- **2 teaspoons red wine (optional)**
- **1 teaspoon bottled minced garlic**
- **3 ½ teaspoons granulated sugar**
- **¼ - ½ teaspoon all-purpose flour**

Make Ahead

Rinse chicken thighs then remove skin place in a plastic bag and add Italian dressing let marinate in refrigerator overnight.

Instructions:

1. Preheat oven on 350 degrees place marinated chicken thighs on a large non-stick baking pan and bake for 40-50 minutes or until cooked all the way through. Once chicken is cooked turn off oven but leave chicken in oven to keep warm.
2. Heat a medium non-stick pan sprayed with no-stick over medium-low heat then adds garlic and cranberries stirring frequently cook for 2 minutes. Add balsamic, sugar and red wine (if using) to pan with cranberries stir everything together let cook for another minute then slow stir in some flour to help sauce thicken once a little thick turn off heat.
3. Remove chicken from oven place on platter and evenly top with each thigh with cranberry sauce then serve.

Turkey & Black Bean Tacos – Makes 8-10 tacos

- **1 pound ground turkey**
- **½ cup can black beans**
- **¼ cup diced yellow onion**
- **3 Tablespoons chopped black olives**
- **¼ teaspoon chili powder**
- **1 ½ packets taco seasoning**
- **¾ cup water**
- **shredded lettuce**
- **bag shredded Colby & jack cheese**
- **8-10 taco shells**

Instructions:

1. In a large pan over medium-high heat cook ground turkey until brown and cooked through then drain any excess grease.
2. Add taco seasoning and water to turkey stirring everything together then add black beans, onion, black olives, and chili powder stirring everything together. Bring mixture to boil then lower heat and simmer for 5-6 minutes stirring occasionally.
3. Remove taco meat from heat and assemble tacos by placing 2-3 tablespoons of taco meat into each shell top with cheese and lettuce then serve.

Mini Turkey Meatloaf's – Makes 4 mini loafs

- 1 pound ground turkey
- ¼ cup diced yellow onion
- ¼ cup diced red bell pepper
- 1 teaspoon bottled minced garlic
- ½ teaspoon hickory smoked salt
- 2 teaspoons Worcestershire sauce
- ½ teaspoon liquid smoke
- 2 Tablespoons yellow mustard
- 1 ½ teaspoons tomato paste
- 1 egg
- 1 Tablespoon brown sugar
- 1 ¼ cup panko bread crumbs
- 1/3 cup bottled BBQ sauce
- dashes ground black pepper

Instructions:

1. In a medium bowl mix together bread crumbs, brown sugar, and hickory smoked salt. Heat a greased medium pan over medium heat then add bell pepper, onion, and garlic let cook for 2-3 minutes stirring frequently. Preheat oven on 350 degrees.
2. In a large mixing bowl add turkey, Worcestershire, liquid smoke, mustard, paste, bread crumb mixture, cooked bell pepper mixture, and egg. Mix everything together thoroughly making sure to all ingredients are mix with turkey meat.
3. Form mini loafs with about ¼ pound of meat mixture and place on a large baking pan sprayed with no-stick then place in oven let bake for 20 minutes. After 20 minutes, evenly baste mini loafs with BBQ sauce then place back in oven continue to cook for 50-60 minutes or until cooked through do not overcook because it will dry out loafs. Remove loafs from oven let set for a minute then serve.

Turkey Parmesan – Makes 4 servings

- **4 turkey cutlets**
- **¼ cup diced yellow onion**
- **¼ cup diced red bell pepper**
- **2 cups bottled plain tomato sauce**
- **1 cup plain panko bread crumbs**
- **½ cup milk**
- **2 eggs**
- **2 teaspoons bottled grated parmesan cheese**
- **1 teaspoon bottled minced garlic**
- **4 sliced provolone cheese**
- **dashes paprika**
- **dashes ground black pepper**

Instructions:

1. Place a turkey cutlet between two sheets of plastic wrap then pound out cutlet start from the center working outwards until thin; repeat with remaining cutlets until all four are done. Preheat oven on 350 degrees.
2. In a shallow dish mix together bread crumbs with paprika, ground black pepper and 1 teaspoon of parmesan cheese. In another shallow dish whisk together milk with egg then take each piece of pounded out turkey cutlet and dip into egg wash then evenly coat with bread crumbs. Place each coated cutlet on a large non-stick baking pan and bake for 25 minutes.
3. While the cutlets are cooking make the sauce, by mixing together tomato sauce, diced onion, diced bell pepper, minced garlic and 1 teaspoon parmesan cheese in a medium pot over low heat. Let sauce simmer for 20 minutes then turn off burner and cover until needed.
4. Once turkey cutlets are done then evenly spoon about ½ a cup of tomato sauce over each cutlet then top with provolone cheese. Place bake in oven to bake for another 10 minutes or until cheese has melted. Remove from heat and serve.

Turkey Wings w/Cranberry Sauce – Makes 4 servings

- 3 ½ -3 ¾ pounds or 4 extra large turkey wings (rinsed)
- 5 cups warm water
- ¼ cup kosher salt
- 7 Tablespoons brown sugar
- 1 ½ cups fresh whole cranberries
- 2 Tablespoons balsamic vinegar
- 2 teaspoons red wine (optional)
- 1 teaspoon bottled minced garlic
- 3 ½ teaspoons granulated sugar
- ¼ - ½ teaspoon all-purpose flour

Make Ahead

Whisk together warm water with kosher salt and brown sugar. Place turkey wings in a large resealable plastic bag then pour water mixture over wings and marinate overnight in the refrigerator.

Instructions:

1. Preheat oven on 325 degrees then discard brine and pat wings dry. Place wings on a large non-stick baking pan. Place in oven let bake for 50-60 minutes then transfer wing to a heat grill and place on direct heat let cook for 10 minutes turning once. Move wings to indirect heat continue to cook for another 15-25 minutes or until wings are cooked through and juices run clear. Remove from heat and keep warm.
2. Heat a medium non-stick pan sprayed with no-stick over medium-low heat then adds garlic and cranberries stirring frequently cook for 2 minutes. Add balsamic, sugar and red wine (if using) to pan with cranberries stir everything together let cook for another minute then slow stir in some flour to help sauce thicken once a little thick turn off heat.
3. Plate turkey wings then evenly top each with cranberry sauce and serve.

Pork Dishes

Grilled Pork Fajitas – Makes 4-6 servings

* 1 ¾ pound boneless pork country style ribs
* 3 Tablespoons package fajita seasoning
* 1 red bell pepper cut into quarters
* 1 cup sliced yellow onion
* 2 tomatoes diced
* 3 Tablespoons olive oil
* 2 teaspoons margarine
* ¼ teaspoon salt
* ¼ teaspoon ground black pepper
* 1 teaspoon bottled lime juice
* ½ teaspoon chili powder
* ½ cup shredded Colby jack
* 1 package of fajita style tortillas

Make Ahead

Sprinkle on each side of boneless ribs fajita seasoning making sure to rub into meat. Place in plastic container and marinate overnight in refrigerator.

One Hour before Grilling

1. Mix together olive oil, salt, and ground black pepper then in a plastic bag place quartered bell pepper and pour olive oil mixture over bell pepper let marinate for one hour in refrigerator
2. In a small plastic container mix diced tomatoes, lime juice, and chili powder together then place in refrigerator to marinate.

Instructions:

1. Preheat grill on medium heat around 375 then place ribs over direct heat then cook for 5 minutes on each side. Move ribs to top rack to finish cooking them over in-direct heat. Cook ribs for 35 minutes on lower heat until no pink in the center turning only once halfway through cooking.

2. Once ribs are moved to top rack then grease a grilling screen and place on bottom rack of grill then add the quartered bell peppers. Cook bell peppers for 15 minutes turning to make sure bell peppers do not burn too much but there should be some char on the bell peppers.
3. Once bell peppers and the boneless ribs are done let rest for 5 minutes. Meanwhile, heat stove burner to medium-high heat and in medium fry pan melt margarine add onions season with a dash of salt and dash black pepper. Cook for 5-7 minutes until onions are golden brown.
4. Slice the ribs into thin slices and slice the bell pepper. Place on table sliced rib meat, sliced bell pepper, cooked onion, shredded cheese, tomato mixture from refrigerator, and tortillas so everyone can build their own fajitas.

Stuffed Peppers – Makes 4 Halves

- ½ pound ground pork
- 1/3 cup cooked instant white rice
- 1 teaspoon can chopped green chilies
- 3 Tablespoons can diced garlic tomatoes
- 3 Tablespoons taco seasoning
- 1 ¾ Tablespoons diced onion
- ½ teaspoon bottle minced garlic
- 1 teaspoon lime juice
- 1 teaspoon chili powder
- 2 slices provolone cheese
- ½ cup water
- 2 large green bell peppers

Instructions:

1. Wash peppers remove tops and seeds then place in a medium pot cover with water and place on medium to high heat. Let peppers boil for about 3-5 minutes or until tender then remove from heat place on paper napkin lined plate to let drain.
2. In a large skillet cook ground pork over medium-low heat until pork is brown and cooked through then stir in taco seasoning and water let simmer for 5 minutes.
3. Remove cook pork from pan and set aside in a medium bowl then add the onion, garlic, chilies, rice, and chili powder to pan let sauté for 1-2 minutes. Return cooked pork to pan and add the tomatoes stirring everything together and cook for another minute.
4. Cut the slices of provolone cheese into thin strips. Preheat oven on 325 degrees then cut peppers in halve lengthwise evenly spoon pork mixture into the 4 halves then top each with strips of provolone. Bake in oven for 5 minutes or until cheese is melted then remove from oven and serve.

Sweet & Sour Pork – Makes 4 servings

- **4 boneless thin pork chops**
- **2/3 cup thinly sliced yellow onion**
- **1 cup can pineapple chunks**
- **½ cup all purpose flour plus ½ teaspoon set aside**
- **2 Tablespoons olive oil**
- **dashes sea salt**
- **dashes ground black pepper**
- **sweet & sour sauce recipe (see page 183)**

Make Ahead

Cut the pineapple chunks in half place in refrigerator until needed. The sweet & sour sauce needs to be doubled for this recipe make sauce ahead of time cover keep warm on low heat.

Instructions:

1. In a medium shallow dish mix flour with salt and pepper set aside then cut pork chops in half then cut into strips should get about 8 strips from each chop. Heat olive oil in a large non-stick pan over medium heat. Dredge pork in flour then add to pan cook for 10-15 minutes turning once halfway through.
2. Once pork is cooked remove from pan then add onion and pineapple to pan let cook for 2 minutes stirring frequently. Add pork, sweet & sour sauce and ½ teaspoon of flour to pan stirring everything together turn heat down let cook for 5 minutes stirring frequently. Remove from heat and serve.

Pork Stir-Fry – Makes 4 servings

- **4 thin boneless pork chops**
- **4 ¼ cups broccoli florets**
- **2 shallots**
- **2 teaspoons bottled minced garlic**
- **1 cup red bell pepper strips**
- **6 Tablespoons Ponzu soy sauce**
- **¼ cup Worcestershire**
- **1 teaspoon hickory liquid smoke**

Make Ahead
> **Whisk together Worcestershire and liquid smoke then place pork chops in a large resealable plastic bag pour Worcestershire mixture over chops and let marinate for 4 hours.**

Instructions:

1. Heat a large non-stick pan sprayed with no-stick over medium heat. Chop up shallots set aside until needed then cut pork into cubes and add to heated pan. Cook pork for 8 minutes then remove from heat set aside.
2. Add chopped shallots, garlic, broccoli, and bell pepper to pan stirring frequently and let cook for 3-5 minutes. Add pork back to pan stirring everything together and add soy sauce to pan stirring everything together let cook for 2-3 minutes. Remove from heat and serve.

Root Beer Ribs – Makes 4 servings

- **8 country style boneless ribs**
- **2 cups root beer**
- **¼ cup fajita seasoning**

Make Ahead

In a medium mixing bowl whisk together root beer and fajita seasoning then place ribs in a gallon size resealable bag pour root beer mixture over ribs. Place in refrigerator overnight to marinate.

Instructions:

1. Heat the grill on medium-high heat discard marinade and place ribs on direct heat for 5 minutes turning once halfway through. Finish ribs on top rack or over in-direct heat for 15-20 minutes or until cooked through remove from heat and serve.

Mini Pork Loaves – Makes 6 loaves

- 1 pound ground pork
- 2 Tablespoons diced sweet onion
- 2 Tablespoons diced red bell pepper
- 1 Tablespoon red wine
- 1 Tablespoon Worcestershire
- 1 teaspoon hickory smoked liquid smoke
- 1 Tablespoon can tomato paste
- 5 Tablespoons plain panko bread crumbs
- 1 teaspoon onion powder
- 1 teaspoon garlic powder
- 2 teaspoons light brown sugar
- ½ teaspoon paprika
- ½ teaspoon salt
- ½ teaspoon ground black pepper
- ½ teaspoon ground mustard
- 3 Tablespoons yellow mustard
- 2 Tablespoons honey
- 1 egg

Instructions:

1. Mix onion powder, garlic powder, brown sugar, paprika, salt, black pepper, and ground mustard in a small bowl and set aside until needed. Preheat oven on 350 degrees.
2. In a large mixing bowl mix together the ground pork, onion, bell pepper, wine, Worcestershire, liquid smoke, and tomato paste. Add bread crumbs, egg, and brown sugar mixture to bowl making sure to thoroughly mix all ingredient with pork.
3. Form 6 mini-loaves out of the pork mixture and place on a medium non-stick baking pan place in oven to bake for 1 hour or until cooked through. In a small mixing bowl whisk together the honey and yellow mustard. After the pork loaves have been baking for 15 minutes, baste each loaf with honey mustard and place back in oven to continue baking. Once hour is up check to make sure cooked through then let rest for 1-2 minutes before serving.

Baked Pork Chops – Makes 4 servings

- **4 thin boneless pork chops**
- **¾ cup Italian dressing**
- **½ instant potato flakes**
- **¼ cup bottled grated parmesan cheese**

Make Ahead
    Marinate pork chops in Italian dressing overnight.

Instructions:

1. Preheat oven on 350 degrees then in a medium shallow dish mix potato flakes with parmesan cheese and set aside. Remove pork chops from marinated shaking off any excess then dredge in potato flakes making sure to cover both sides. Place breaded pork chops on a medium baking pan sprayed with no-stick.
2. Place in oven to bake for 25-30 minutes or until cooked through then remove from heat and serve.

Teriyaki Pork Chops w/Pineapple Chutney – Makes 4 servings

- **4 thick boneless pork chops**
- **1 cup teriyaki sauce**
- **¾ cup pineapple juice**
- **¾ cup can crushed pineapple (drained)**
- **¼ cup diced red bell pepper**
- **¼ cup diced shallots**
- **4 teaspoons apple cider vinegar**
- **1 teaspoon cornstarch**
- **2 teaspoons pineapple juice**

Make Ahead

Whisk together teriyaki sauce with ¾ cup pineapple juice set aside then butterfly each pork chop and place pork chops in a large resealable plastic bag pour teriyaki sauce over chops. Place marinating chops in refrigerator for 8 hours.

Instructions:

1. Heat a large non-stick pan over medium-low heat add bell pepper and shallots let cook for 2-4 minutes stirring occasionally then stir in crushed pineapple and apple cider vinegar. Let cook for 5 minutes stirring occasionally. Whisk together cornstarch and 2 teaspoons pineapple juice then add slurry to pan stirring everything together continue to cook for a minute or until mixture starts to thicken. Remove pan from heat then cover to keep warm while grilling the pork chops.
2. Heat grill on medium-high heat drain pork chops and add to grill let cook for 10-12 minutes or until preferred doneness turning only once. Remove chops from heat plate and evenly top each with pineapple chutney and serve.

Ham Steak w/Cranberry Chutney – Makes 1 ham steak

- 1 large fully cooked ham steak
- ½ cup orange juice
- ½ teaspoon brown sugar
- 1 teaspoon Dijon mustard
- ¼ teaspoon all-purpose flour
- 1 cranberry chutney recipe (see page 189)

Make Ahead

In a small mixing bowl stir together orange juice, brown sugar, Dijon mustard, and flour until brown sugar and flour are absorbed. In a container or plastic bag place ham steak with orange juice mixture and let marinate in refrigerator for 4 hours.

Instructions:

1. Heat large non-stick pan over medium-low heat then cook ham steak for 10-15 minutes or until ham is cooked through turning once halfway through.
2. Remove from heat then thinly slice ham and serve with cranberry chutney.

Honey Mustard Ham Steaks – Makes 4 ham steaks

- 4 (6ounce) fully cooked ham steaks
- ¼ cup Dijon mustard
- 3 ½ Tablespoons honey

Tip

The ham steaks can be grilled instead of pan-fried. Follow instructions but instead of cooking in a pan cook on grill over medium-low heat basting through out cooking. Cook for 5-6 minutes or until some char starts to appear turning once halfway through cooking.

Instructions:

1. Whisk together Dijon and honey then baste ham steaks both sides set aside. Heat a large non-stick pan over medium heat and add the ham steaks two at a time. Cook for 6-8 minutes turning once halfway through then remove from heat and serve.

Section 5

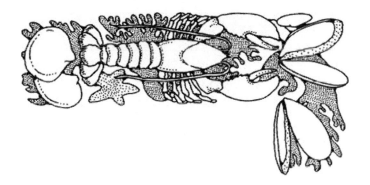

Seafood
&
Fish

Seafood

Lobster Tacos – Makes 4-6 tacos

- 4 (5ounce) lobster tails
- 1 tomato broth recipe (see page 176)
- 4-6 fajita size tortilla
- 2/3 cup diced tomato
- ½ cup shredded lettuce
- 1 teaspoon lime juice
- 1 teaspoon chili powder
- 2/3 cup diced Avocado

Instructions:

1. Mix diced tomatoes, lime juice, and chili powder together then chill.
2. Steam lobster tails shell part down in tomato broth over medium heat for about 8-10 minutes or until meat turns opaque and shells turn a bright reddish color.
3. Take lobster meat out of tails and cut up *(tail meat should be cut up in cubes)*
4. Put meat into tortilla making sure there is an equal amount in each tortilla then top with shredded lettuce, diced tomato mixture, and avocado then serve.

Grilled Shrimp Tacos – Makes 4-6 serving

- **1 pound raw jumbo Shrimp (veins removed and shells removed including tail shells)**
- **2 ½ teaspoons fajita seasoning**
- **4-6 taco size tortillas**
- **¾ cup shredded lettuce**
- **avocado salsa recipe (see page 188)**

Make Ahead

Rinse shrimp then pat dry place in refrigerator until needed. Season shrimp with fajita seasoning; seasoning both sides then place in plastic bag or container and refrigerate for 4-6 hours. Make Avocado salsa ahead of time and place in refrigerator until needed.

Instructions:

1. Heat grill on medium heat. Grill shrimp on direct heat* for 6-7 minutes on each side or until opaque and cooked through.
2. Place 4-6 shrimp in each into tortillas then top with lettuce and a teaspoon of avocado salsa then serve

*Using a greased grill screen usually makes grilling shrimp easier

Shrimp Fajitas – Makes 6 fajitas

- **24 extra large raw shrimp (veins removed and shells removed including tail shells)**
- **1 ½ teaspoons mesquite liquid smoke**
- **1 Tablespoon Worcestershire**
- **1 Tablespoon fajita seasoning**
- **¾ cup thinly sliced yellow onion strips**
- **¾ cup thinly sliced red bell pepper**
- **¾ cup shredded lettuce**
- **1 Tablespoon olive oil**
- **6 whole wheat fajita size tortillas**
- **dashes sea salt**
- **dashes ground black pepper**

Make Ahead

Rinse shrimp pat dry then in a small bowl whisk together liquid smoke, Worcestershire and fajita seasoning pour mixture into a bag and add shrimp. Make sure all shrimp get covered with fajita seasoning mixture let marinate in refrigerator for 4-6 hours.

Instructions:

1. In a large non-stick pan heat olive oil over medium-high heat; add onion and bell pepper to pan season with salt and ground pepper cook for 2 minutes.
2. Add shrimp to pan stirring everything together cook for 5-6 minutes or until shrimp are opaque. Remove shrimp mixture from heat serve with tortillas and lettuce.

Shrimp-Stir Fry – Makes 2-4 servings

- 1 pound large raw shrimp (veins removed and shells removed including tail shells)
- 1 ½ cup sliced sweet onion
- 1 cup red bell pepper strips
- 1 can baby corn (drained)
- 4 teaspoons bottled minced garlic
- ¾ cup soy sauce
- 2 ½ Tablespoons basting teriyaki sauce
- 1-1 ½ Tablespoons all-purpose flour
- ¼ cup oil

Instructions:

1. Rinse shrimp then pat dry place in refrigerator until needed. Heat oil over medium-low heat in a large skillet then add the onion and bell pepper sauté for 2-3 minutes then add the garlic and sauté for another minute. Next, add the shrimp and baby corn sauté for a minute then lower heat to low and cover.
2. Continue to cook for 5-6 minutes or until shrimp is opaque then uncover turn heat back up to medium-low. Add the teriyaki and soy sauce stir everything together and sauté for another 1-2 minutes.
3. Finally, slowly add flour stirring into shrimp mixture until it dissolves and sauce starts to thicken remove from heat and serve over white rice.

Lemon Shrimp Stir-Fry – Makes 3-6 servings

- **30-35 extra large raw shrimp (veins removed and shells removed including tail shells)**
- **1 cup fresh snow peas**
- **½ cup red bell pepper strips**
- **½ cup yellow onion strips**
- **1 teaspoon bottled minced garlic**
- **1 teaspoon lemon pepper seasoning**
- **1 Tablespoon olive oil**
- **1 lemon sauce recipe (see page 180)**

Instructions:

1. Rinse shrimp pat dry season each shrimp on both sided evenly with 1 teaspoon lemon pepper seasoning. Rinse snow peas removing tips and strings set as until needed.
2. In a large non-stick pan heat olive oil over medium-low heat then add the seasoned shrimp; cook shrimp for 3-4 minutes or until opaque making sure to turn over to cook both sides then remove shrimp from pan and set aside.
3. Add the bell pepper, onion, snow peas and garlic to pan stirring occasionally and cook for 3-4 minutes; add shrimp back to pan stirring everything together continue to cook for another minute or two then add the sauce to pan. Bring to boil stirring frequently continue to cook for another minute or until sauce starts to thicken a little remove from heat and serve.

Shrimp w/Pasta – Makes 4-6 servings

- **20 extra large raw shrimp (shells removed including tail shells and veins removed)**
- **¼ cup diced yellow onion**
- **¼ cup diced red bell pepper**
- **¼ cup diced tomato**
- **1 cup bag baby spinach (rinsed & stems removed)**
- **1 teaspoon lemon pepper seasoning**
- **2 teaspoons bottled minced garlic**
- **2 teaspoons bottled lemon juice**
- **1/3 cup white wine**
- **2 ½ cups low sodium chicken broth**
- **1 ¾ cup uncooked bow tie pasta**
- **2 Tablespoons margarine**
- **dashes sea salt**
- **dashes ground black pepper**
- **dashes dried oregano**
- **dashes garlic powder**
- **dashes onion powder**

Instructions:

1. In a medium pot over high heat bring chicken broth to boil then stir in bow tie pasta turn heat down to medium-low and let pasta boil for 10-15 minutes or until pasta is fork tender. Drain pasta making sure to reserve 1/3 cup of chicken broth then set pasta and broth aside until needed. Add a little oil to pasta so it does not stick.
2. Season shrimp with lemon pepper seasoning. Heat a large non-stick pan over medium heat then add shrimp; cook for 5-7 minutes or until shrimp turn opaque remove from heat chop cooked shrimp up and set aside.
3. Add the onion, bell pepper, garlic, and tomato to the pan cook for 2-3 minutes. Add lemon juice, white wine, reserved chicken broth, margarine and shrimp to pan

stirring everything together cook for 1-2 minutes stirring frequently.

4. Add pasta to pan stirring everything together then add spinach, garlic powder, onion powder, salt, oregano and black pepper to pan stirring everything together let cook for another minute then remove from heat and serve.

Sweet & Sour Grilled Shrimp w/Pineapple Relish – Makes 4 servings

- **20 extra large raw shrimp (shells removed including tail shells and veins removed)**
- **6 Tablespoons can crushed pineapple**
- **¼ cup diced tomato**
- **2 teaspoons bottled lime juice**
- **½ teaspoon bottled dried mint flakes**
- **½ sweet & sour recipe (see page 183)**

Tip

This recipe requires only ½ of the sweet & sour recipe which should be made right before grilling shrimp.

Make Ahead

In a medium mixing bowl mix together pineapple, tomato, lime juice, and mint flakes and chill for 2 hours before serving.

Instructions:

1. Once sweet & sour sauce is made set aside until needed. Rinse shrimp pat dry then once shrimp are ready use a small amount of sweet & sour sauce to baste one side of shrimp. Place shrimp in refrigerator until ready to cook.
2. Heat grill on medium-high heat and spray a grill screen with no-stick then place on grill let screen warm up for about a minute then add shrimp. Be careful because shrimp could stick so make sure screen is sprayed well. Once shrimp are on the grill let grill for 5-8 minutes or until shrimp are opaque turning once halfway through. Use the rest of the sweet & sour sauce to baste shrimp while grilling making sure to generously baste each side of each shrimp.
3. Once shrimp are cooked remove from heat then plate shrimp by evenly placing some pineapple relish in the middle of each plate and surround with 5 shrimp each then serve.

Crab Cakes - Makes 4 cakes

- **1 can lump crab meat**
- **1 egg**
- **¼ teaspoon salt**
- **2 teaspoons fine diced medium sweet onion**
- **2 teaspoons fine diced red bell pepper**
- **1 teaspoon lemon juice**
- **dashes ground red pepper**
- **½ teaspoon Worcestershire sauce**
- **½ teaspoon dry mustard**
- **1/3 cup dry bread crumbs (2 tablespoons extra set aside on a plate)**
- **2 Tablespoons butter**

Instructions:

1. In a medium mixing bowl stir together salt, onion, bell pepper, lemon juice, ground red pepper, Worcestershire, and dry mustard.
2. Slowly fold crab meat into mixture then slowly stir in the egg as well which will help bind the mixture together. Slowly fold the bread crumbs into the crab mixture.
3. Make four balls out of mixture then press to form cakes. Heat 2 tablespoons of butter in a cast iron skillet over medium heat.
4. Take formed cakes and dredge in the extra tablespoons of bread crumbs that where set aside earlier. Once all four cakes have been dredge through then add to hot skillet.
5. Cook for about 2-3 minutes on each side or until they are golden brown. Remove from heat and serve.

Pasta with clams – Makes 4-5 servings

- 3 ½ cups uncooked bow tie pasta
- 2 (6.5ounces) can minced clams (drained reserving 1 ½ tablespoon clam juice)
- ½ cup diced fully-cooked andouille sausage
- ½ cup bag baby spinach
- 2/3 cup cherry tomatoes
- 1/3 cup diced red bell pepper
- 1/3 cup diced yellow onion
- 2 teaspoons bottled minced garlic
- 1 ½ Tablespoons olive oil
- 2 teaspoons lemon juice
- 4 ½ cup water
- dashes salt
- dashes ground black pepper
- dashes ground oregano

Make Ahead

Rinse spinach and remove stem. Rinse cherry tomatoes then quarter then place both spinach and tomatoes in refrigerator until ready to use.

Instructions:

1. Bring 4 ½ cups of water to boil in a medium pot then add pasta turn heat down to medium-low let boil for 10-12 minutes or until pasta is fork tender. Drain pasta then set aside.
2. In a large pan heat ½ tablespoon of olive oil over medium-low heat; add andouille sausage, onion, bell pepper, and garlic cook for 4-5 minutes stirring frequently.
3. Add clams to pan continue to cook for 3-4 minutes then add pasta, clam juice, lemon juice, salt, pepper, oregano, tomatoes, and spinach stirring everything together continue to cook for 2-3 minutes. Remove from heat then serve.

Seared Scallops w/White Wine Sauce – Makes 4 servings

- **12 raw colossal sea scallops**
- **1 teaspoon lemon-pepper seasoning**
- **1 ¼ Tablespoons white wine (cooking wine)**
- **2 teaspoons bottled lemon juice**
- **2 Tablespoons margarine**
- **2 teaspoons bottled minced garlic**
- **dashes sea salt**
- **dashes ground black pepper**

Instructions:

1. Heat a large non-stick pan sprayed with no-stick over medium heat; evenly season scallops with lemon-pepper seasoning then add to pan cook for 2 minutes on each side then cover let cook for 8-10 minutes or until scallops become opaque.
2. Remove scallops from pan. Set aside on large shallow platter. Add margarine, white wine, lemon juice and minced garlic season with salt and pepper stirring everything together let cook for 1-2 minutes then pour over scallops and serve.

Honey-Mustard Scallops w/Black Bean Relish – Makes 4 servings

- 12 raw colossal sea scallops
- 1 cup honey
- 1 ¼ cup Dijon mustard
- 1 cup can black beans
- ½ cup can corn
- 8 cherry tomatoes
- 1 Tablespoon bottled lime juice
- 1 Tablespoon chili powder

Make Ahead

In a medium mixing bowl whisk together honey and mustard set aside. Rinse scallops then pat dry and place in a large resealable bag add honey-mustard mixture to bag making sure to cover all scallops. Place in refrigerator to marinate for 6 hours.

Instructions:

1. Rinse tomatoes then dice up set aside until needed. In a medium mixing bowl stir together the black beans, corn, tomatoes, lime juice and chili powder then place in refrigerator until needed.
2. Heat grill on medium-high heat then spray a grill screen with non-stick place on grill over direct heat. Place scallops on grill screen use tongs to move scallops back and forth for a few minutes so that do not stick to screen.
3. Let scallops cook for 10-15 minutes or until cooked through and opaque turning only once halfway through cooking time. Turn grill off remove scallops. Plate scallops on a platter then evenly top each with black beans relish and serve.

Fish

Cajun Catfish – Makes 2-4 servings

- **1 pound catfish**
- **¼ cup all-purpose flour**
- **3 Tablespoons Cajun seasoning**
- **3 Tablespoons oil**

Tip

To test oil place a small piece of bread into oil to see if it floats and starts to cook or sprinkle a little flour to see if it starts to fizz and cook.

Instructions:

1. Heat oil in a cast iron skillet over medium heat. Evenly season catfish with 1 ½ Tablespoon Cajun seasoning on both sides.
2. In a shallow bowl mix flour and 1 ½ Tablespoon of Cajun seasoning. Once oil is heated coat catfish with flour on both sides adds to heated oil.
3. Cook for 10-12 minutes or until cooked through turning once halfway through. Drain cooked fish on paper towel before serving.

Tuna Steaks w/Lemon Sauce – Makes 4 tuna steaks

- **4 raw tuna steaks**
- **2 Tablespoons olive oil**
- **salt**
- **ground black pepper**
- **½ lemon sauce recipe (see page 180)**

Instructions:

1. Heat a greased or non-stick large pan over medium heat. Baste tuna steaks evenly with olive oil on both sides then evenly season each with salt and ground black pepper.
2. Place seasoned tuna steaks in heated pan cook for 10 minutes or until cooked through and flakes easily.
3. Remove cooked tuna steaks place on platter then evenly drizzle each with lemon sauce and serve.

Tuna Steaks w/Avocado Relish – Makes 4 tuna steaks

- **4 raw tuna steaks**
- **2 teaspoons lemon-pepper seasoning**
- **1 Tablespoon olive oil**

Avocado Relish
- **2 avocado**
- **¼ cup diced tomato**
- **2 Tablespoons diced yellow onion**
- **2 Tablespoons diced red bell pepper**
- **1 ¼ Tablespoons bottled lime juice**
- **½ teaspoon dried mint leaves**

Make Ahead

Cube avocado then mixing with rest of relish ingredients in a medium mixing bowl careful not to break up the avocado cubes. Place in refrigerator for 2 hours before serving.

Instructions:

1. Heat olive oil over medium heat in a non-stick pan; evenly season each piece of tuna with lemon-pepper seasoning then place in heated pan. Cook tuna for 10 minutes or until cooked to desired temperature turning once halfway through cooking.
2. Remove tuna from pan place on a platter then evenly top each piece of tuna with avocado relish and serve.

Tuna Salad Stuffed Shells – Makes 5 stuffed shells

- **1 (4.5ounce) packet of hickory smoked tuna**
- **1 Tablespoon diced white onion**
- **4 cherry tomatoes**
- **¼ cup bag baby spinach**
- **3 teaspoons light mayo**
- **dashes paprika**
- **dashes ground black pepper**
- **5 uncooked extra jumbo pasta shells**
- **½ lemon sauce recipe (see page 180)**

Tip

Make the lemon sauce first then cover and keep warm on very low heat.

Instructions:

1. Remove stems and rinse baby spinach place in a large bowl. Rinse the cherry tomatoes then dice and add to bowl with spinach. Add tuna, mayo, and onion to bowl with spinach mixing everything together then season with ground black pepper and paprika. Place tuna mixture in refrigerator until needed.
2. In a medium pot bring about 2 cups of water to boil then add the jumbo shells turn heat down to medium-low. Let pasta boil for 15-20 minutes or until tender.
3. Drain pasta then rinse will some cool water to cool pasta. Take each pasta shell and stuff with around 1-1½ Tablespoons of tuna mixture into each shell drizzle each shell with lemon sauce then serve.

Tuna Cakes – Makes 6 tuna cakes

- **2 (2.6 ounces) packets of plain tuna**
- **¼ cup diced cherry tomatoes**
- **¼ cup diced yellow onion**
- **½ teaspoon lemon pepper seasoning**
- **2 Tablespoons light mayo**
- **½ teaspoon lemon juice**
- **dashes ground black pepper**
- **6 Tablespoons plain bread crumbs**

Instructions:

1. Pre heat oven on 350 degrees. In a large mixing bowl mix together the first seven ingredients then slowly mix in the bread crumbs one tablespoon at a time.
2. Once all ingredients are mixed together then form the cakes there should be six cakes when finished. Place finished tuna cakes on a medium non-stick baking pan then put in oven and cook for 25-30 minutes turning once halfway through. Once finished cooking remove from and serve.

Lemon-Pepper Crusted Cod – Makes 4 crusted fillets

- **4 fresh cod fillets**
- **2/3 cup plain bread crumbs**
- **1 ¼ Tablespoons lemon pepper seasoning**
- **¼ cup milk**
- **1 egg**
- **2 teaspoons bottled lemon juice**

Instructions:

1. Preheat oven 350 degrees. In a medium shallow dish mix together bread crumbs and lemon pepper seasoning set aside. In another medium shallow dish whisk together milk, egg, and lemon juice.
2. Dip cod fillet in the egg mixture shaking off any excess then dredge through bread crumb mixture coating each side; Repeat with remaining cod fillets.
3. Place coated cod fillets on a large baking pan sprayed with no-stick and place in oven to bake for 30-35 minutes or until cod is cooked through and flakes easily with a fork. Remove from heat and serve.

Citrus Cod w/Pineapple Chutney – Makes 4 servings

- **4 fresh cod fillets**
- **1 cup can pineapple chunks**
- **2 ½ Tablespoons reserved can pineapple juice**
- **¼ cup diced yellow onion**
- **¼ cup diced red bell pepper**
- **2 teaspoons cornstarch**
- **2 ¼ teaspoons apple cider vinegar**
- **¼ cup bottled lemon juice**
- **¼ cup bottled lime juice**
- **¼ cup bottled honey**
- **¼ teaspoon chili powder**

Make Ahead
In a medium bowl whisk together lemon juice, lime juice, chili powder and honey place cod in a large resealable bag then pour lemon juice mixture over cod let marinate in refrigerator for 4 hours.

Instructions:

1. Preheat oven on 325 degrees then place cod on a large baking pan sprayed with no-stick and bake for 30-25 minutes or until fish is cooked through.
2. Meanwhile, heat a large non-stick pan sprayed with no-stick over medium-low heat add onion and bell pepper let cook for 1-2 minutes then add pineapple juice, pineapple chunks, cider vinegar and cornstarch stirring everything together let cook for 1 minute. Once cod is done remove from oven evenly top with pineapple chutney and serve.

Tilapia w/Dijon Sauce – Makes 4 servings

- **2 pounds tilapia**
- **2/3 cups low-sodium chicken broth**
- **1 Tablespoon all-purpose flour**
- **1 Tablespoon margarine**
- **¼ cup Dijon mustard**
- **2 Tablespoons olive oil**
- **ground black pepper**
- **dashes paprika**

Instructions:

1. In a medium pot melt margarine over low heat whisk in flour then add broth whisking everything together and bring to boil. Lower heat whisk in Dijon and paprika then turn off burner and cover sauce.
2. Heat oil in a large pan over medium-low heat then evenly season the tilapia with ground black pepper on both sides. Add tilapia to pan let cook for 12-15 minutes or until tilapia is cooked through turning once halfway through.
3. Once tilapia is done plate and evenly top tilapia with Dijon sauce and serve.

Lemon-Pepper Tilapia w/Tomato Relish – Makes 4 servings

- 1 ½ pound tilapia or 4 large fillets
- 1 teaspoon lemon-pepper seasoning
- 10 cherry tomatoes
- 2 Tablespoons diced yellow onion
- 2 Tablespoons diced green bell pepper
- ½ teaspoon chili powder
- 1 Tablespoon bottled lime juice

Make Ahead

Rinse cherry tomatoes then chop up. In a medium bowl mix together cut-up tomatoes, onion, bell pepper, chili powder and lime juice. Let relish chill in refrigerator at least 3-4 hours before using.

Instructions:

1. Preheat oven on 325 degrees then evenly season tilapia with lemon-pepper seasoning place on a large baking pan sprayed with no-stick. Bake tilapia for 23-30 minutes or until cooked through and flaky.
2. Remove cooked tilapia from oven then evenly top with tomato relish and serve.

Pan-fried Tilapia w/Garlic-Lemon Sauce – Makes 4 servings

- **2 pounds fresh tilapia or 8 tilapia fillets**
- **¾ cup bottled lemon juice**
- **2 lemons**
- **2 teaspoons bottled minced garlic**
- **3 Tablespoons margarine**
- **2/3 cup all-purpose flour**
- **dashes sea salt**
- **dashes ground black pepper**
- **dashes paprika**

Tip

This recipe will need to be cooked in batches so add more margarine if needed as needed.

Instructions:

1. Zest the two lemons set aside until needed then using medium shallow dish season flour with salt, pepper, and paprika. Heat a large pan over medium-low heat adds 2 Tablespoons of margarine. Pat fish dry then dredge in flour place in pan to cook for 10-12 minutes or until tilapia is cooked through. Repeat with remaining tilapia.
2. Once tilapia is finish cooking add 1 Tablespoon margarine to pan let melt then add garlic, lemon juice, and lemon zest to pan stirring everything together let cook for a minute stirring frequently. Plate tilapia then pour sauce over tilapia and serve.

Lemon-Pepper Crusted Halibut w/Mushrooms – Makes 4 servings

- **4 raw halibut fillets**
- **1 ¼ cup plain panko bread crumbs**
- **4 teaspoons lemon-pepper seasoning**
- **2 Tablespoons dry white wine (cooking wine)**
- **2 (7ounce) can sliced mushrooms**
- **2 Tablespoons bottled lemon juice**
- **1 teaspoon bottled minced garlic**
- **2 shallot cloves**
- **2 teaspoons lemon zest**
- **2 eggs**
- **2 Tablespoons low-fat milk**
- **dashes sea salt**
- **dashes ground black pepper**

Instructions:

1. In a medium shallow dish whisk together eggs with milk set aside and using another medium shallow dish mix together bread crumbs with lemon-pepper seasoning set aside.
2. Preheat oven on 325 degrees. Dip halibut fillets into egg mixture covering both sides then dredge in bread crumbs covering both sides place on a large baking pan sprayed with no-stick. Bake halibut for 30-40 minutes or until cooked through and flaky.
3. The last 8 minutes of baking start the mushrooms by heating a medium non-stick pan sprayed with no-stick over medium heat then finely dice shallots. Add minced garlic as well as diced shallot to pan let cook for 2 minutes stirring occasionally. Add the mushrooms to the pan stirring together continue to cook for 4 minutes then add wine, lemon juice, and zest to pan stirring everything together continue to cook for another 2 minutes or until liquid is absorbed making sure to stir occasionally.
4. Once halibut is done then plate and evenly top each with mushrooms then serve.

Section 6

Sides
&
Sauces

Sides

Au Gratin Potatoes – Makes 4-8 servings

- **3 baking potatoes**
- **½ cup plain bread crumbs**
- **3 Tablespoons melted butter**
- **Three cheese sauce recipe (see page 118)**
- **dashes of paprika**

Instructions:

1. Preheat oven 325 degrees then grease a 6x9 glass casserole pan.
2. Mix melted butter with bread crumbs and set aside. Peel and wash potatoes then thinly slices each potato.
3. Stir potatoes into three cheese sauce. Pour potato and cheese mixture into glass casserole pan
4. Add the bread crumbs on top making sure to cover the whole top with bread crumbs then add the dashes of paprika. Bake for about 35-40 minutes then let sit 5 minutes before serving.

Sour Cream & Onion Potatoes – Makes 2-4 servings

- **1 ¼ pound of white potatoes**
- **3 Tablespoons sour cream & onion seasoning**
- **3 Tablespoons melted margarine or butter**

Instructions:

1. Preheat oven on 350 degrees. Wash potatoes then cut into large cubes and put into a plastic resealable bag.
2. Add melted butter to bag then close bag and shake. Add sour cream and onion seasoning to bag with potatoes and butter then close and shake again making sure potatoes are covered with seasoning.
3. Pour potatoes into large non-stick baking pan then bake for 50-60 minutes or until fork tender and remove from oven let sit for 5 minutes before serving.

Mashed Potato Pancakes – Makes 9 pancakes

- **1 large baking potato**
- **¼ cup ranch seasoning**
- **1 Tablespoon bottled grated parmesan cheese**
- **1 Tablespoon fat free milk**
- **2 teaspoons margarine**

Instructions:

1. Peel the potato rinse then cut into cubes place cube potatoes into a medium pot cover with water. Bring water to boil over medium-high heat turn heat down once potatoes start to boil then continue to boil for 15-20 minutes or until potatoes are fork tender stirring occasionally.
2. Drain potatoes then place in a large mixing bowl using a fork mash potatoes then add ranch seasoning, milk, parmesan cheese and margarine mixing everything together.
3. Take 1 Tablespoon of potato mixture and form patties then cook over medium-low heat in a large non-stick pan for 6 minutes turning once halfway through. Remove from pan and serve.

Twice Baked Potatoes – Makes 4 potatoes

- **2 baking potatoes**
- **4 strips of cooked turkey bacon**
- **3 Tablespoons ranch seasoning**
- **2 Tablespoons no-fat cream cheese**
- **1 teaspoon margarine**
- **¼ cup low-fat milk**

Instructions:

1. Rinse potatoes then with a fork poke lots of holes in each potato both sides making sure to pierce the meat of the potato this will keep it from exploding in the microwave then microwave for 5 minute intervals on medium-low heat.
2. Once the potato is a little soft felling remove from microwave and let stand for 5-8 minutes or until potato is cool enough to handle.
3. Preheat oven on 325 degrees. Cut each potato in half lengthwise then using a spoon scoop out the pulp of each potato leaving a thin amount of pulp in the potato shell.
4. Place removed pulp into a medium mixing bowl then add ranch seasoning, margarine, cream cheese, and milk mixing everything together then crumble in bacon stirring everything together.
5. Take the potato mixture and evenly spoon into potato shells once all four shells are filled then place on a small greased baking pan and put in oven let bake for 20 minutes. Remove from oven let set for 5 minutes then serve.

BBQ Potatoes – Makes 3-4 servings

- 2 white potatoes (rinsed & diced)
- 3 Tablespoons diced sweet onion
- 3 Tablespoons diced green bell pepper
- 4 strips cooked turkey bacon
- 1 Tablespoons olive oil
- 1 ½ Tablespoons yellow mustard
- 1 Tablespoon ketchup
- 1 teaspoon tomato paste
- ½ teaspoon paprika
- 1 teaspoon garlic powder
- 1 teaspoon onion powder
- salt
- ground black pepper

Tip

During the first 20 minutes of cooking the potatoes more olive oil may needed to add slowly at a time to help keep potatoes from drying out.

Instructions:

1. Dice cooked turkey bacon set aside until needed then rinse and cube potatoes. In a large non-stick heat olive oil over medium-low heat then add potatoes season with salt and pepper.
2. Cook potatoes for 20 minutes stirring occasionally then add the rest of the ingredients stirring everything together let cook for 10 minutes then cover and continue to cook for 15-20 minutes or until potatoes are fork tender. Remove from heat season with salt and pepper as needed then serve.

Glazed Carrots – Makes 4 servings

- **1 cups of bag baby carrots (rinsed)**
- **½ cup margarine or butter**
- **½ cup light brown sugar**
- **1 ½ Tablespoons yellow mustard**

<u>Instructions:</u>

1. Melt margarine in microwave then in a small bowl whisk together margarine, brown sugar, and mustard until sugar has dissolved set aside.
2. Heat a greased medium pan or non-stick pan over medium-low heat and add baby carrots cook for 6-9 minutes or until carrots are fork tender.
3. Add margarine mixture to carrots and let cook for another 2-3 minutes continually stirring. Remove from heat and serve

Mushrooms – Makes 4-6 servings

- **2 cups fresh sliced button mushrooms (rinsed)**
- **2 teaspoons bottled minced garlic**
- **1 Tablespoon bottled lemon juice**
- **2 Tablespoons red wine**
- **1 Tablespoon margarine**
- **dashes salt**
- **dashes ground black pepper**

Instructions:

1. In a large pan over medium heat melt margarine then add mushrooms seasoning with salt and pepper cook for 6-8 minutes stirring occasionally.
2. Add garlic, lemon juice, and red wine to mushrooms stirring everything together and cook for another 3-5 minutes stirring occasionally or until mushrooms start to caramelize then remove from heat and serve.

Orange Broccoli – Makes 4 servings

- **2 ½ cup broccoli florets (rinsed)**
- **½ cup orange juice**
- **3 Tablespoons margarine**
- **3 Tablespoons orange zest**

Instructions:

1. Melt margarine in a large non-stick pan over medium heat then add broccoli cook for 2-3 minutes stirring occasionally. Add orange juice as well as orange zest to pan stirring everything together let cook for another 2-3 minutes or until broccoli is fork tender stirring frequently. Remove from heat and serve.

Grilled Eggplant – Makes 4 servings

- **1 eggplant**
- **¼ cup olive oil**
- **½ teaspoon garlic powder**
- **½ teaspoon onion powder**
- **¼ teaspoon hickory smoked salt**
- **½ teaspoon paprika**
- **¼ teaspoon ground black pepper**
- **2 teaspoons light brown sugar**

Instructions:

1. In a small bowl mix together garlic powder, onion powder, salt, paprika, pepper, and brown sugar set aside. Rinse eggplant then cut off both end and discard. Cut eggplant into ½ inch-1 inch rounds should get around 9-10 rounds out eggplant.

2. Heat grill on high heat. Evenly baste each round both sides with olive oil then evenly season each round both sides with brown sugar mixture. Rub seasoning into rounds on both side then place on grill over direct heat. Grill eggplant for 8-12 minutes or until eggplant is soft in the center. Remove from heat and serve.

Snow Peas & Tomatoes – Makes 4 servings

- **4 cups fresh snow peas**
- **2 cups cherry tomatoes**
- **¼ cup olive oil**
- **¼ cups balsamic vinegar**
- **2 teaspoons bottled minced garlic**
- **dashes salt**
- **dashes ground black pepper**

Instructions:

1. Wash tomatoes then cut in half and put the halved tomatoes in a bowl and place in refrigerator until needed. Wash snow peas then remove tips and strings.
2. In a medium non-stick pan heat olive oil over medium-low heat and garlic let cook for a few seconds continually stirring. Add snow peas to pan stirring together with garlic and olive oil season with salt and ground black pepper. Cook snow peas for 3-5 minutes stirring frequently.
3. Add tomatoes and balsamic vinegar to pan stirring everything together and continue to cook for another minute. Remove from heat and serve.

Vegetable Stir-Fry – Makes 3-4 servings

- **2 cups fresh broccoli florets**
- **2 cups fresh sliced button mushrooms**
- **½ cup fresh snow peas**
- **½ cup yellow onion strips**
- **½ cup red bell pepper strips**
- **3 Tablespoons olive oil**
- **2 Tablespoons soy sauce**
- **2 ½ Tablespoons orange juice**
- **1 teaspoon bottled minced garlic**
- **dashes ground black pepper**

Tip

Rinse snow peas, broccoli, red bell pepper, and mushrooms before preparing or slicing.

Instructions:

1. Remove stems and strings from snow peas. In a large fry pan heat olive oil over medium-low heat add all the vegetables. Cook vegetables for 5 minutes stirring frequently then add garlic, soy sauce, orange juice, and black pepper stirring everything together.
2. Continue to cook for 1-2 minutes stirring frequently then remove from heat and serve.

Chorizo Stuffing- Makes 4-8 servings

- ½ pound regular pork chorizo
- ½ cup diced yellow onion
- ¼ cup diced green bell pepper
- 1 teaspoon bottled minced garlic
- ½ cup low-sodium chicken broth
- 1 sourdough roll diced up-dried
- 3 Tablespoons grated Parmesan
- ½ teaspoon ground black pepper
- 1 egg

Instructions:

1. Preheat oven 350 degrees then grease a 6x9 glass casserole pan. Mix in a large bowl the bread, parmesan, and black pepper and set aside.
2. Over medium heat in a medium pan cook the chorizo for 20 minutes then add to the pan the onion, bell pepper, and garlic continue to cook for 10 minutes constantly stirring.
3. Add the cooked vegetables & chorizo mixture, chicken broth, and egg to the bread and parmesan mixture and toss together. The egg will act as a binder to hold everything together.
4. Place stuffing mixture into glass casserole pan cover with foil bake for 20-25 minutes then take foil bake for another 10-15 minutes until golden brown. Let set for 5 minutes then serve.

Turkey Stuffing – Makes 4-6 serving

- ½ package turkey breakfast sausage
- ½ cup diced yellow onion
- ¼ cup diced green bell pepper
- ¼ cup chopped fresh button mushrooms
- 1 teaspoon bottled minced garlic
- ½ cup low-sodium chicken broth
- 1 sourdough roll diced up-dried
- 3 Tablespoons grated Parmesan
- ½ teaspoon ground black pepper
- 1 egg

Instructions:

1. Preheat oven 350 degrees then grease a 6x9 glass casserole pan. Mix in a large bowl the bread, parmesan, and black pepper and set aside.
2. Over medium heat in a medium pan cook turkey sausage about 15-20 minutes or until brown and cooked through. Remove sausage from pan let sit until cool enough to touch then dice sausage and place back in pan.
3. Add to the pan the onion, bell pepper, mushrooms, and garlic continue to cook for 10 minutes constantly stirring.
4. Add the sautéed vegetables & sausage mixture, chicken broth, and egg to the bread and parmesan mixture and toss together. The egg will act as a binder to hold everything together.
5. Place stuffing mixture into glass casserole pan cover with foil bake for 20-25 minutes then take foil bake for another 10-15 minutes until golden brown. Let set for 5 minutes then serve.

Fried Rice – Makes 3-6 servings

- ¾ cup cooked white rice
- 2 eggs
- ¾ cup cooked top sirloin steak diced
- ½ cup chopped broccoli
- ¼ cup diced yellow onion
- ¼ cup diced can carrots
- 2 Tablespoons soy sauce
- 2 Tablespoons garlic teriyaki sauce
- 2 Tablespoons oil

Instructions:

1. Heat oil in large pan over medium-low heat then add onions and carrots cook for 5 minutes.
2. Add the rice to pan stir together cook for 3 minutes then add the broccoli, steak, soy sauce, and teriyaki sauce stir together and let cook for 5 minutes.
3. In a small separate pan cook the 2 eggs making sure to scramble them once cook add cooked eggs to rice mixture. Stir cooked eggs into rice mixture then serve.

Spanish Rice – Makes 2-6 servings

- **2/3 cups dry instant white rice**
- **2/3 cups water**
- **3 Tablespoons diced white onion**
- **3 Tablespoons diced red bell pepper**
- **½ teaspoon bottled minced garlic**
- **½ cup can diced tomatoes**
- **2 Tablespoons non-chunky salsa**
- **2 teaspoons chili powder**
- **1 teaspoon lime juice**
- **¼ teaspoon salt**
- **Dashes green hot sauce**

Instructions:

1. Heat a greased medium pan or non-stick pan over medium-low heat then add onion, bell pepper, chili powder, and garlic sauté for 1-2 minutes.
2. Then add rice, water, tomatoes, salsa, lime juice, salt, and hot sauce stir everything together turn heat down to low and cover.
3. Continue to cook for 10-15 minutes or until water has been absorbed stirring occasionally. Remove from heat leave covered and let stand for 2 minutes then serve.

Mushroom Rice – Makes 2-6 servings

- ¾ cup brown instant rice
- 8 fresh white button mushrooms
- ½ teaspoon bottled minced garlic
- ½ teaspoon bottled lemon juice
- 1 teaspoon white wine
- ¾ cup low-sodium beef broth
- 1 ½ Tablespoon soy sauce
- 1 ½ Tablespoon Worcestershire
- 1 teaspoon margarine
- dashes salt
- dashes ground black pepper

Instructions:

1. In a small pot bring broth to boil over medium-high heat then stir in rice turn off heat cover rice let sit for 5 minutes or until water is absorbed and rice is fluffy.
2. Remove stems from mushrooms then rinse and place on a plate covered with a paper towel to drain. Chop up mushrooms set aside.
3. Melt margarine in a medium pan over medium-low heat then add mushrooms and season with salt and black pepper cook for 1-2 minutes. Add garlic to mushrooms continue to cook for another minute.
4. Add wine and lemon juice to the pan with mushrooms then continue to cook for 2-3 minutes. Once mushroom have finished cooking stir them into the pot with the cooked brown rice along with soy sauce and Worcestershire then season with salt and black pepper stirring everything together and serve.

Onion Straws- Makes 2 – 4 serving

- 1 egg
- ¼ cup milk
- 3 ounces all-purpose flour
- 2 Tablespoons ranch seasoning
- 3 Tablespoons of oil
- ½ yellow onion

Tip

To test oil place a small piece of bread into oil to see if it floats and starts to cook or sprinkle a little flour to see if it starts to fizz and cook

Instructions:

1. Cut onion into thin strips set aside. Preheat oil on medium-low heat in a medium pan.
2. Whisk egg and milk together and pour into a shallow bowl. Mix flour and ranch seasoning into another shallow bowl.
3. Once oil is heated dip the thin strips of the onion in the egg mixture then dip in flour mixture coating completely.
4. Add to heated oil cook for 3-5minutes turning to make sure both sides are cooked. Drain on paper towel then serve.

Egg Noodles – Makes 2-4 servings

- **2 cups water**
- **2 chicken bouillon cubes**
- **1 cup egg noodles**
- **2 ½ teaspoons of margarine**
- **¼ teaspoon of black pepper**

Instructions:

1. Bring to boil 2 cups of water then add the 2 chicken bouillon cubes stirring until cubes are absorbed. Add noodles to broth and let boil on medium-low heat for 10-15 minutes or until noodles are soft making sure to stir occasionally.
2. Once noodles are done drain then pour noodles into a mixing bowl and add the margarine and black pepper tossing everything together and serve.

Garlic Pasta – Makes 4 servings

- 1/3 box of angel hair pasta
- 1 Tablespoon bottled minced garlic
- 1 Tablespoon minced shallot
- 4 Tablespoons olive oil
- 1 Tablespoon margarine
- 1 Tablespoon bottled grated parmesan cheese
- 1 Tablespoon sour cream
- dashes sea salt
- dashes ground black pepper
- dashes Italian seasoning
- dashes garlic powder
- dashes onion powder
- 5 cups water

Instructions:

1. Bring 5 cups of water to boil in a medium pot then add pasta let cook for 10-12 minutes or until pasta is tender.
2. The last few minutes of the pasta boiling heat 1 Tablespoon of olive oil in a large pan over medium-low heat add garlic and shallots let cook for a minute stirring frequently. Drain pasta then add to pan with remaining olive oil, margarine, parmesan, sour cream, salt, pepper, Italian seasoning, garlic powder and onion powder stirring everything together let cook for 1-2 minutes stirring frequently. Remove from heat and serve.

Baked Beans – Makes 1 ¾– 2 cups

- 1 (15.5ounce) can red beans
- ¼ cup diced yellow onion
- 1 ½ Tablespoon yellow mustard
- ¼ cup ketchup
- 1 ½ teaspoon honey
- 1 ¼ Tablespoon brown sugar
- 4 slices turkey bacon
- ½ teaspoon tomato paste
- dashes ground black pepper

Instructions:

1. In a medium pan over medium heat cook turkey bacon for 6-7 minutes or until bacon is crisp turning frequently remove from pan set aside to let cool. Once cool then crumble up bacon and set aside.
2. Heat a medium pot over medium-low heat then add bacon and onion to pot cook for 2-3 minutes stirring frequently. Drain about a teaspoon of liquid from can of beans then add the beans with rest of liquid to pot stirring everything together.
3. Add mustard, ketchup, honey, brown sugar, tomato paste, and ground black pepper stirring everything together then bring mixture to a boil stirring frequently.
4. Once mixture starts to boil then turn heat down to low cover and let simmer for 50 minutes stirring occasionally. After 50 minutes, remove from heat and let sit for 5 minutes before serving.

Sauces

Tomato Broth – Makes 1 ½ - 1 ¾ cups

- 1 can diced tomato
- 1 ½ cups chicken broth
- 1 teaspoon bottled minced garlic
- dash of salt
- dash of ground black pepper

Tip

Great sauce to serve over fish or seafood as well as steam shellfish

Instructions:

1. Sauté minced garlic in medium pan for about 1 minute then add the rest of ingredients.
2. Simmer for about 5 minutes on low heat. Remove from heat and serve.

Southwest Tartar Sauce – Makes 1 cup

- 1 cup mayo
- ¼ cup diced dill pickles
- 1 ½ Tablespoons chopped sweet onion
- 1 teaspoon dried parsley
- 1 teaspoon bottled lemon juice
- ¼ teaspoon Worcestershire sauce
- 3 Tablespoons chili powder
- 3 Tablespoons ground red pepper
- dashes of hot sauce

Instructions:
1. Mix all ingredients in a medium mixing bowl then chill before serving.

Three Cheese Sauce – Makes 1-1 ½ cups

- **6 slices of white American cheese sliced into strips**
- **¾ cup shredded Colby & jack cheese**
- **¼ cup grated parmesan**
- **1 Tablespoon butter**
- **1 Tablespoon all-purpose flour**
- **¾ cup milk**

Instructions:

1. In a small sauce pan over low heat melt 1 Tablespoon of butter once melted whisk in a Tablespoon flour and keep whisking until it is a golden color.
2. Stir in milk then stir in all three cheese making sure to whisk everything together then turn up the heat to medium to help melt the cheese keep whisking so sauce does not burn.
3. Sauce will thicken up as it starts to boil once it starts to boil turn heat down to very low heat and let simmer for about 5 minutes whisking occasionally.
4. Turn off the burner and let sauce sit for 5 minutes then serve. It is great over potatoes or vegetables.

Brown Sauce – Makes 1-1 ½ cups

- **2 Tablespoons butter**
- **2 Tablespoons all-purpose flour**
- **2 ½ Tablespoons soy sauce**
- **2 teaspoons Worcestershire**
- **1 cup beef broth**

Instructions:

1. In a small sauce pot over low heat melt butter and once melted whisk in flour continually whisk until turns a light brown color.
2. Once a light brown color whisk in broth, soy sauce, and Worcestershire then continually whisk until sauce start to thicken then remove from heat let stand for a minute before using. Great for steak dishes.

Lemon Sauce – Makes 1 1/3 -1 ½ cup

- **(1 1/3) cup chicken broth**
- **4 teaspoons all-purpose flour**
- **4 teaspoons margarine**
- **2 teaspoons soy sauce**
- **¼ lemon juice**

Instructions:

1. Melt margarine over low heat in a small pot once margarine is melted stir in the flour. Continually stir flour and margarine until flour is absorbed.
2. Add chicken broth, lemon juice, and soy to the pot stirring everything together. Turn up the heat to medium-low and let boil for 1-2 minutes stirring frequently once it has thicken up a little remove from heat and serve. Great for chicken, fish, and seafood dishes.

Orange Sauce – Makes 1-1 ½ cups

- **1 cup chicken broth**
- **½ cup orange juice**
- **1 teaspoon soy sauce**
- **2 Tablespoons margarine or butter**
- **2 Tablespoons all-purpose flour**

Instructions:

1. In a small pot over low heat melt margarine then add flour whisking together then whisk in chicken broth.
2. Turn heat up to medium-low then add stir in orange juice and soy sauce bring to low boil stirring frequently then remove from heat and add to poultry or pork dishes.

Dijon Sauce – Makes 2/3 – 1 cup

- 2/3 cups low-sodium chicken broth
- 1 Tablespoon all-purpose flour
- 1 Tablespoon margarine
- ¼ cup Dijon mustard
- dashes paprika

Instructions:

1. In a small pot melt margarine over low heat whisk in flour then add broth whisking everything together and bring to boil. Lower heat whisk in Dijon and paprika remove from heat and serve.

Sweet & Sour Sauce – Makes ¾ cup – 1 cup

- ¾ cup pineapple juice
- 1/3 cup ketchup
- 1 ½ teaspoons soy sauce
- 1 ½ teaspoon granulated sugar
- 1 ½ teaspoon apple cider vinegar
- 1 ½ teaspoon tomato paste
- dashes sea salt
- dashes ground black pepper

Instructions:

1. In a small pot whisk all the ingredients together then bring to boil stirring frequently once sauce starts to boil turn heat down to low and let simmer for 1-2 minutes stirring occasionally. Remove from heat and serve.

BBQ Sauce – Makes 2/3 – ¾ cup

- **2/3 cup ketchup**
- **½ cup apple cider vinegar**
- **2 teaspoon Worcestershire**
- **1 teaspoon mesquite liquid smoke**
- **¼ cup diced yellow onion**
- **1 ¼ Tablespoons brown sugar**
- **1 teaspoon tomato paste**
- **2 teaspoon margarine**
- **dash salt**
- **dash ground black pepper**

Instructions:

1. Melt margarine in a small pot over low-medium heat add onion season with salt and pepper let onion cook for 1 minute stirring frequently. Add to the pot the ketchup, vinegar, Worcestershire, liquid smoke, sugar and tomato paste whisking everything together.
2. Turn heat up to bring sauce to boil stirring frequently then turn heat down to low and let simmer for 10-15 minutes stirring occasionally. Remove from heat and serve.

Light Chunky Tomato Sauce – Makes 1-1 1/3 cups

- **2 Tablespoons olive oil**
- **1 teaspoon bottled minced garlic**
- **2 teaspoons diced yellow onion**
- **½ cup can diced garlic & olive oil tomatoes (3 teaspoons reserved juice)**
- **¼ cup can black beans**
- **dashes dry ground oregano**
- **dashes salt**
- **dashes ground black pepper**

Instructions:

1. Heat olive oil in a medium pan over medium-high heat then add onion and garlic let sauté for 1-2 minutes.
2. Add tomatoes, oregano, and salt, pepper, beans, and tomato juice stirring everything together then bring to boil. Once mixture starts to boil turn heat down to low and let simmer for 5-8 minutes stirring occasionally. Remove from heat and serve great for pasta dishes.

Sausage Country Gravy – Makes 1 – 1 ½ cups

- 1 package maple flavor sausage breakfast links
- 2 Tablespoons butter
- 1 ½ Tablespoons all-purpose flour
- 1 cup of milk
- ¼ teaspoon salt
- 1 teaspoon ground black pepper
- ½ teaspoon paprika

Tip

Omitting the sausage make this the perfect country gravy to put over country fried steak.

Instructions

1. In a small fry pan cook sausage over medium-low heat until they are a crispy brown and cooked all the way through *(make sure to brown every side of the sausage)*. Once cooked remove from heat and let cool.
2. Reserve about 1 ½ teaspoon of sausage drippings from the pan. Once sausage has cooled then dice up into very small pieces and set a side.
3. In a small sauce pot melt the butter and whisk in the flour into the melted butter. Keep whisking together until the rue turns a golden brown color.
4. Once the rue is a golden brown color add the milk, salt, paprika, and pepper and keep whisking everything together over medium-high heat until the mixture starts to bubble.
5. Once it starts to bubble add the diced sausage and turn the heat down to low to let the mixture thicken. Once thicken remove from heat and serve over biscuits.

Vinaigrette Dressing – Makes ½ - ¾ cups

- ½ cup olive oil
- 3 oz red wine vinegar
- 1 teaspoon Italian seasoning
- 1 teaspoon bottled minced garlic
- 1 Tablespoon bottled lemon juice
- 2 Tablespoons Dijon mustard
- Dashes of salt
- Dashes of black pepper

Instructions:

1. In a mixing bowl add ingredients and whisk together for a minute to make sure everything is mix together then it is ready. Great for salads or sandwiches.

Avocado Salsa – Makes 2-4 servings

- **1 avocado**
- **3 ounces cherry tomatoes – rinsed & quartered**
- **3 Tablespoons diced medium sweet onion**
- **3 Tablespoons diced red bell pepper**
- **2 teaspoons lime juice**
- **½ teaspoon chili powder**
- **¼ teaspoon salt**
- **½ teaspoon green hot sauce**

Instructions:

1. Cut avocado into small cubes then in a medium mixing bowl add all ingredients and mix together *(be careful not to break up the cubes of avocado because the salsa should be chunky)*.
2. Chill for at least 4-6 hours before serving.

Cranberry Chutney – Makes ½ cup - 1 cup

- **1 cup fresh whole cranberries**
- **1 Tablespoon granulated sugar**
- **¼ cup white vinegar**
- **2 Tablespoons diced yellow onion**
- **2 Tablespoons diced red bell pepper**
- **1 teaspoon cornstarch**
- **2 Tablespoons orange juice**

Instructions:

1. Rinse cranberries then cut in half and set aside. Heat a greased medium pan medium-low heat then add onions and bell pepper and sauté for 2-3 minutes.
2. Add cranberries continue to sauté for 2-3 more minutes then add the sugar and vinegar continue to cook for 2 minutes
3. In a small bowl combine orange juice and cornstarch whisk until smooth. Add orange juice mixture to cranberry mixture and bring to low boil and cook for another 3 minutes. Remove from heat and serve. Great for pork or poultry dishes.

Cherry Sauce – Makes ½ cups

- ½ cup dried cherries
- ½ teaspoon bottled minced garlic
- 3 Tablespoons balsamic vinegar
- ¼ cup red wine
- 1 teaspoon granulated sugar
- dashes salt

Instructions:

1. Chop up dried cherries set aside. Heat a greased medium pan or non-stick pan over medium-high heat adds the garlic and cherries cook for 2-3 minutes stirring frequently.
2. Turn heat down to medium-low add balsamic vinegar, red wine, salt, and sugar to pan stir everything together and let simmer for a few minutes or until liquid starts to reduce. Once reduces remove from heat serve with poultry or pork dishes.

BBQ Rub – Makes 1/3 cup

- **2 Tablespoons paprika**
- **2 Tablespoons light brown sugar**
- **1 teaspoon garlic powder**
- **1 teaspoon onion powder**
- **½ teaspoon ground mustard**
- **½ teaspoon ground black pepper**
- **½ teaspoon hickory smoked salt**

Instructions:

1. Mix all ingredients together in a container for up to a month. Great for chicken or pork dishes.